THE FENG SHUI
OF GARDENING

THE FENG SHUI OF GARDENING

Philippa Waring

SOUVENIR PRESS

First published 1998 by
Souvenir Press Ltd,
43 Great Russell Street, London WC1B 3PA

ISBN 0 285 63436 4

Typeset by Rowland Phototypesetting Ltd,
Bury St Edmunds, Suffolk

Printed in Great Britain by
The Guernsey Press Co. Ltd., Guernsey, Channel Islands

In China, the endeavour is to keep in close
touch with the beauties of nature as a divine
and beneficent influence.
H. N. Wethered, horticulturist, 1933

Feng Shui says that a beautiful garden is like
the clothes of a house.
Wong Siew Hong, xiansheng, 1997

CONTENTS

ACKNOWLEDGEMENTS

In writing this book I have been very fortunate to have the help and guidance of several experts who not only assisted me with their own knowledgeable opinions on the subject, but also made available (and where necessary translated) a number of Oriental texts and documents on the practice of horticulture in China. Among those I can name are Jiang Ping Jie, Kwok Man Ho and Wong Siew Hong who were my teachers as I studied the philosophies of Feng Shui in relation to the garden. I should also like to thank several Western gardening authorities who have particularly interested themselves in Chinese horticulture, including A.W. Anderson, Eric Maple, Frederick Shepherd, Professor Richard Bernard, Alan Macdonald, John Brooks and D. G. Turner; and my thanks to David Higham Associates for permission to quote from *Penny Foolish* by the late Sir Osbert Sitwell. Once again I am grateful to my publishers for all their help during this, my second excursion into one of the world's oldest, most mysterious, yet universal arts.

PW

PREFACE

Feng Shui gardening is not the latest horticultural fad. It is probably the oldest form of garden cultivation in the world, dating back several millennia to a time when China, where it first evolved, was already well on the way to becoming a great civilisation while we, in the West, were still a largely barbaric people.

It is based upon the simple philosophy that man and nature must live in harmony with one another and that all life is infused with an invisible energy which the Chinese named *Chi*. This force circulates throughout the environment and is essential to our well-being, health and happiness. As *The Book of Lao Tzu* has described the creation of all things: 'The pure and light *Chi* rose to become heaven, the muddy and heavy fell to become earth; the breath which harmoniously blended both became man.' In simple terms, man's place was midway between heaven and earth, united with everything else in existence by this essence called *Chi*.

The Chinese sages who devised Feng Shui believed that any man-made feature—building, shrine, grave or garden— could affect the flow of this beneficial energy, and they consequently established the rules of placement that are central to their philosophy. Everything must be correctly shaped and situated to ensure the smooth flow of the *Chi*.

A garden could be no exception, and it was here, as a result of careful observation and a painstaking study of nature, that these wise men came to appreciate that there were things such as rocks, water, pathways, and a number of flowers, plants and trees, which could assist the channelling and promotion of the *Chi* energy for the benefit of those who lived on the property. The result of their deliberations was the Chinese Feng Shui garden.

It should be understood right from the outset that the Feng Shui garden is rather different from our accepted ideas of gardening in the West. It is not like a country cottage garden, nor does it have a formal layout of the kind favoured in towns and cities. In this garden balance and harmony are the key factors, regardless of size or location, for even in ancient China properties ranged from sprawling estates to small plots—just as they do today. The value of a piece of land on which to relax, grow some suitable flowers and plants and maybe even a tree, was governed not merely by its size. It is a concept that is as relevant and applicable today as it was then.

This balance and harmony can only be achieved by a careful attention to detail, however. The Chinese talk of all life as a balance between *Yin* and *Yang* (to which I shall return later in the book), two interdependent universal forces which must have each other in conjunction to achieve their effect. To put this in context: your home or flat, which is made of bricks, concrete, steel, wood, nails and other solid construction materials, is *Yang,* while the earth, rocks, pond, plants, flowers and trees of the garden are *Yin.* By creating a balance between the two you allow the *Chi* to circulate easily; and where this is at present not occurring, I hope that this book will enable you to put it right and by so doing enhance your life as well as the enjoyment you get from your garden.

There are certain basic truths about the Feng Shui of gardening that will become apparent as you read the book:

1 The key is to try to make everything look as *natural* as possible. No matter whether it is the plants you are growing or the features you have created, nothing should look contrived.

2 A vital element of balance is to mix the *shapes* and *sizes* of your plants so that no one item or group overwhelms any other. Massed beds of colourful flowers may be favoured in Western gardens, but according to Feng Shui *subtlety*, with a few delicate colours and plenty of green leaves, is a far better conductor of the *Chi*.

3 *Paths* are an essential part of any garden, and where we in the West have usually laid them in straight lines to get from one place to another as quickly as possible, this is a dangerous shape in Feng Shui and should be replaced by a gently curving or winding pathway that will facilitate the passage of the natural energy.

4 A Feng Shui garden must *never be crowded*. Centuries ago the Chinese decided that a more relaxing and harmonious place could be created by carefully siting a few complementary flowers, plants and trees, and allowing room for other important elements such as a pond, rock garden and even a small herb bed.

5 Despite the impression often given that the Chinese prefer exotic plants and flowers—an idea probably fostered by the tales of excited early visitors to the mysterious country, describing 'a fairyland of colourful flowers'—a few recommended Feng Shui plants are actually more important to achieve the desired effect. In a sentence: *balance and harmony are all.*

For a good many years now there has been a vogue for Japanese gardening in the West. But it has to be said that the philosophy behind it actually came to Japan from China—although the Japanese subsequently developed along their own lines, evolving their own distinctive garden style, and have probably now surpassed their teachers as florists. However, in view of the dramatic increase of interest in Feng Shui in the West, it is surely high time to focus on the ancient

A traditional Feng Shui garden, complete with water feature, rockery, trees and flowers, from an old Chinese engraving.

principles themselves and follow the Feng Shui guidelines to achieve a better garden.

There is much to be said for a practice that can generate natural energy and vitality in a garden, as well as enabling a gardener to create a unique and peaceful plot wherever he or she may live. The principles hold true even where there is no more than a tiny patio available. By practising what the ancient Chinese learned more than three thousand years ago, everyone today can enhance not only the environment in which they live but, especially, their own joy and sense of well-being.

So, happy Feng Shui gardening!

Philippa Waring
Suffolk, Spring 1998

1 SUCCESSFUL GARDENING THE FENG SHUI WAY

When David and his wife, Anne, bought their semi-detached house on a suburban estate, they did so because they liked the look of the property and because there was a convenient train service to London where David had a new job. They both knew the house would need a few things doing to it—painting and redecorating, perhaps some modifications and maybe even an extension later on—but they could see themselves making it a happy home for their two boys, Chris and Tom.

Today they admit that they did not pay a great deal of attention to the garden when viewing the house, as neither considered themselves then to be keen gardeners. In fact, the plot was fairly basic, in the style of many suburban properties. While they were being shown round, they did notice that the owner had put most of the rear garden down to lawn, run a concrete path down one side, and planted a very mixed selection of flowers in two borders along each fence. There was also a small vegetable patch and a compost heap at the bottom of the garden.

In the months following their move, David and Anne did little more than keep the lawn mown and the beds reasonably tidy, and plant a few vegetables, while devoting most of their energies to the house. It was not until the next summer, when they felt settled in the house, that they really had a chance to take stock of their surroundings. Unbeknown to each other, they both began to feel that, despite the contentment they felt *inside* their home, the gardens at front and rear were, frankly, depressing. Indoors, they had managed to create a comfortable environment for themselves and the boys, but as soon as any of them went out into the garden their spirits seemed to fall and they felt no inclination to stay there. The garden was simply failing to give the necessary lift to mind and spirit.

Each morning, as Anne looked out of the back windows, she experienced a sense that amounted almost to hopelessness. The same thing happened when she went out of the front door and up the path that ran straight to the front gate between two patches of lawn. It all seemed very unsatisfactory, and she began to worry that somehow the happiness of their home was in danger of being undermined by what she saw as the 'sadness' or lack of vitality of the garden.

It was then that she first read in a magazine about Feng Shui. Anne said later that she was intrigued by what it claimed the ancient Chinese art could do for a house, but what really caught her interest was a statement that Feng Shui regarded the garden as equally important for the well-being, health and prosperity of the owners of a property. The article told her that it was as essential to enhance the environment *outside* a house as it was inside the four walls.

Anne read more about the subject and finally raised the matter with David. He at once admitted that he had also been feeling the garden was a bit of a downer, but had been avoiding the issue rather than make Anne feel he did not like the house. With this realisation, he was keen to learn what Anne had discovered about Feng Shui. And although both now confess that they were initially a little sceptical about the relevance of an art developed in China thousands of years ago, they decided to consult a Feng Shui expert, or *xiansheng*, about their house and garden. What they learned from the visit of this man—and what subsequently transpired when they followed his advice—proved to the couple that their feelings about the garden had indeed been well founded.

The *xiansheng*, a Chinese immigrant from Hong Kong, first explained to David and Anne that it was important for energy to flow smoothly throughout a house and garden. To begin with, he said, the property was facing in an auspicious direction (the south-east) and there were no overly harmful influences in the neighbourhood such as a T-junction or pylons. In the house, however, he suggested rearranging the furniture in several rooms, placing mirrors in the hallways and a wind chime near the front door, all in order to promote the flow of the helpful energies which he referred to as *Chi*. In the couple's bedroom he pointed out that the bed was wrongly positioned to encourage this natural force and in all probability was making the room a harbour for the harmful energy known as *Sha*. This would certainly not enhance the harmony of their relationship.

After making a number of other suggestions about colour schemes and the use of certain ornaments in the kitchen, living-room and bathroom, the Feng Shui expert requested that they all go into the garden. Here he walked around silently for some minutes before beginning to list the faults which he said were causing the whole area to become a battleground between the good *Chi* and bad *Sha* and the major source of the lack of vitality. It was not just that the garden lacked imagination in its layout: a number of elements were directly affecting its harmony.

The straight path from the house to the end of the garden, for instance, was taking the *Chi* directly out of the house and through the garden without giving it any chance to spread its energy. One of the flowerbeds was also in quite the wrong position to help the flow of the earth energies, and very few of the flowers growing in the other bed were particularly good conductors of *Chi*. The vegetable patch was in a detrimental position, and the weeds growing in the unused area were also generating *Sha*. A dying tree in one

SEMI-DETACHED HOUSE - BEFORE

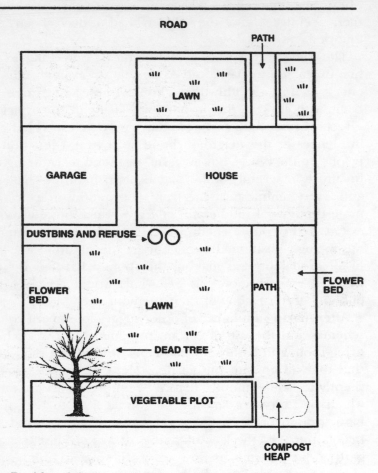

How David and Anne used Feng Shui to transform the
suburban garden of their semi-detached house.

corner, moss in the lawn, and the unsightly compost heap
at the end of the garden, were all contributing towards
making the *Chi* energy stale and the balance and harmony
of the place virtually nonexistent. No wonder they felt
depressed when they were out here, the man said solemnly.

David and Anne carefully noted down everything the consultant told them. To counter their problems, he first recom-

SEMI-DETACHED HOUSE - AFTER

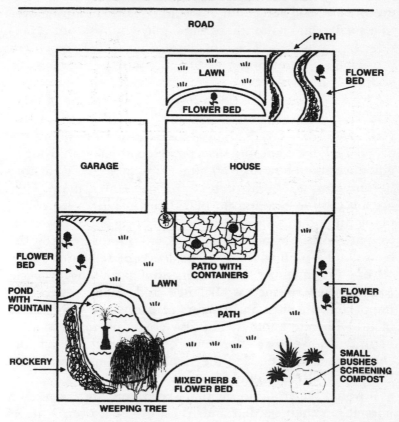

mended that they make a curve in their path to slow down the flow of the *Chi* out of the garden. And because water and rocks are essential elements of Feng Shui, he suggested building a small pond with a fountain and a little rock garden. The dying tree must go at once, and in its place they should plant a typical Feng Shui tree like a willow. Trellis should be erected to support some climbing plants like wisteria or jasmine, because these would improve both the look of the garden and the circulation of the *Chi*. He also recommended that, rather than the vegetable plot, they should create a herb garden with a selection of the plants especially recommended by Feng Shui, a list of which he gave them. The spot where the dustbins stood was another eyesore and bad Feng Shui. It would be far better given over to a small stone patio where the family could sit out peacefully on sunny days. The bins he recommended keeping in the garage where there was ample room, even when the couple's car was inside.

The *xiansheng* left David and Anne with dozens of ideas clamouring in their minds. What he had told them not only confirmed what they had already come to know about the power of Feng Shui, but also provided them with a lot of guidance about how to go about making their garden a more harmonious, not to say prettier and pleasanter, place. They lost no time in drawing up plans and making a list of the plants and flowers they would need to bring about this transformation. All the time, at the back of both their minds, the consultant's parting words of advice kept repeating themselves—to remember that in Feng Shui gardening, *simplicity* was the key to success. Balance and subtlety were all-important: the sizes and colours of plants not only had to blend with one another, but also create an impression of naturalness. Nature's energy was omnipresent, he had concluded; it merely needed the right conditions in which to function to greatest effect.

It would be wrong to say that David and Anne worked a miracle on their garden and transformed it overnight. As they discovered, creating a good Feng Shui garden requires a lot of thought, careful planning and hard work, as well as patience while the new features are introduced and the plants, trees and flowers begin to grow and start performing their appointed task of channelling the flow of *Chi* and deflecting the bad *Sha*. So where the couple had previously been losing energy because of the straight path, they built a graceful, winding gravel replacement. The whole of one corner became a goldfish pond and rockery, while to screen the compost heap they introduced some shrubs, and the vegetable patch became an attractive and fragrant herb bed. The plans of the garden reproduced here show how David and Anne completely revitalised their property: apart from enhancing their lifestyle, they actually made it a much easier garden to maintain.

*   *   *

When Amanda, a young computer systems analyst, moved into her ground floor terraced flat, she already knew about Feng Shui. Indeed, she had picked the four-roomed property with its through lounge/dining room, bedroom, bathroom and kitchen, because of its south-facing aspect and the fact that the interior would be comparatively easy to reorganise to meet the requirements of the ancient art. This she accomplished during the spring months after she took possession.

But once established, like David and Anne she felt something was still not right. Her use of placement, redecoration, mirrors and little ornaments had given the flat good Feng Shui, but the rear of the property still left her with a sense of unease that she could not put down to her neighbours or even the garden itself. She decided to call in the Feng Shui expert she had consulted for her previous flat and get his advice. On his arrival, the *xiansheng* only needed a few minutes to tell Amanda that, indeed, her problem lay in the back garden.

He pointed out that it was all straight lines and cul-de-sacs which were harbouring bad *Sha*. The high brick walls made the whole area rather dark and gloomy, and with a cracked and broken path that ran a few yards straight to the end of the garden, there was nothing to encourage the flow of *Chi*. The square of lawn had no features at all, and many of the plants that Amanda had been nurturing in the L-shaped flowerbed were actually weeds. There was not a tree or shrub in the whole garden, and the general effect was claustrophobic and depressing.

First of all, the *xiansheng* said, Amanda must tackle the bleak walls. He recommended a series of gently undulating bamboo screens to mask the bricks and create an impression of space—certainly of greater privacy. A small ornamental tree such as a flowering cherry would be ideal for the left-

GROUND FLOOR FLAT - BEFORE

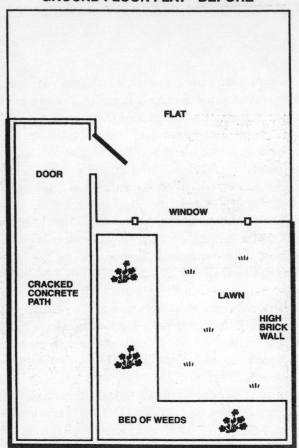

Feng Shui turned the garden of Amanda's ground floor flat into a haven of peace and harmony.

hand corner, while a pathway winding to the other corner, with a small water feature such as a fountain, would attract *Chi* and wildlife. The little lawn only required re-turfing, but the earth energies would flow more smoothly if some strongly perfumed plants and flowers were grown in the flowerbed.

The *xiansheng* felt that a stone patio running round from the back door to the area in front of the lounge/dining-room

GROUND FLOOR FLAT - AFTER

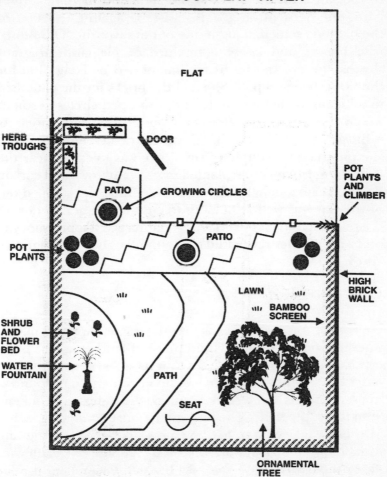

window would provide a harmonious spot in which Amanda could relax. She should group some pot plants at intervals on this, with a climber at the junction of the flat and the wall. Lastly, he suggested a 'love seat' at the far end of the garden, and recommended one of the old-fashioned S-shaped seats on which a couple could sit side by side.

Inspired by this advice, Amanda spent the weekends of the following summer putting the garden to rights, helped by specialists for the work on the patio and winding garden path. She decided on growing wisteria against a section of the bamboo screen, bought one of her favourite 'Old Blush' rose bushes and chose a mixture of pleasantly fragrant shrubs, flowers and herbs recommended by Feng Shui for the flowerbed and pots. She had the bricks for the patio laid in a herringbone pattern, leaving two open circles of soil in which she could plant flowers to soften the whole area. As a finishing touch, to make the most of her limited space, she purchased a couple of small troughs to stand near the back door, in which she planted sage, pennyroyal and coriander to create a delightful aroma every time she stepped out of the flat—as well as helping to sustain the gentle flow of the property's *Chi*. A year later, Amanda was happily showing off to friends her revitalised garden, full of beauty, fragrance and harmony.

*   *   *

Of course, no two gardens are the same. And no matter whether you start with a virgin piece of land on a new property, or tackle a neglected plot that has grown up around an older house—not forgetting the small gardens to be found at the rear of flats and terraced houses–the philosophy of Feng Shui is just the same. The ancient art *can* and *does* work, and in these pages I hope to show how, like David, Anne and Amanda, you too can work this bit of Chinese magic on your own property, *wherever* you may happen to live.

2 THE SECRET OF 'WIND AND WATER'

Feng Shui evolved over three thousand years ago, as a result of the Chinese people's observation of nature and their landscape. Its very name, *Feng Shui*, refers to two of the essential elements of life, wind and water, and it has been described by some modern authorities as 'the electricity of nature'. Whether it is a true art or just a mixture of superstition and folklore as its detractors claim, the extraordinary growth in the popularity of Feng Shui in the late twentieth century owes much to its sensitivity towards the environment as well as to its philosophy of harmony between people and their surroundings in order to foster good health, happiness and prosperity.

Of course, wind and water are not just central to Feng Shui. As every gardener knows, they are equally important in the successful cultivation of flowers, plants and trees—which is one of the reasons why Feng Shui found a place in the lives of those who created China's gardens centuries ago. Those sages carefully developed it into a horticultural art form—a virtual 'science' according to its most enthusiastic advocates—that can be utilised just as effectively in our part of the world today.

We know that the ancient Chinese civilisation first began to develop on the vast central plain which extends from the foothills of the Himalayas in the west to the shores of the Pacific in the east. It was here, roughly on the 40° line of latitude that also runs through Greece, southern Italy, Spain and the southern states of America, that the scattered inhabitants began to come together and formed one of the world's first great civilisations. It would be wrong to imagine that the area was a kind of Garden of Eden—the rains were erratic in summer and in winter the plains could be cold and dusty—but the soil certainly had the capability to nurture a wide variety of trees, plants, flowers and herbs which could sustain mankind. The cultivation and propagation of all these plants made the plains-dwelling Chinese some of the world's first agriculturalists and later gardeners, a people who cherished plant life and venerated what they conceived as the 'gods of vegetation'. Wiser men then began to examine the importance of the environment and man's relationship to it. They sensed an energy driving everything, themselves included, and gradually evolved a way of life they called Feng Shui to capitalise on this power in nature.

Westerners encountering Feng Shui for the first time tend to be rather baffled by the whole concept. All the more so because the enigmatic Chinese liken it to the elements of wind and water 'because no one fully understands that the wind and water cannot be grasped'. At its most basic it is a practice that has grown out of a very close study of the relationship between man, nature and the heavens, benefiting from generations of experience to show that those who live in tune with their environment can significantly enrich their lifestyle and enhance their chances of personal fulfilment.

Natural science developed in China along quite different lines from those of the West. Rather than carrying out practical tests and conducting experiments in the pursuit of scientific knowledge, the ancient Chinese scorned the use of knives and instruments and recorded only what they *observed*. The result was a body of knowledge that combined ancient traditions with inner consciousness. In fact, this radical form of science produced a number of discoveries years ahead of more orthodox experimentation—including the earth's natural energy forces which were much later proved to be the planet's magnetic field.These forces they described as the 'breath of life' and named them *Chi* (pronounced 'Chee').

According to the Chinese, this energy force animates *everything*—the world we live in, all that lives and grows upon it, and, of course, ourselves. The *Chi* is, however, invisible to the naked eye and cannot be heard, felt, touched or tasted. Yet it is what binds everything together, flowing above and below the ground, in water, through rocks and the air itself, and influencing every aspect of man's life in the environment. Quite simply, *Chi* was the most important aspect of the Feng Shui philosophy and the key to harmonious existence. The old sages agreed that it was the spirit that imbued our world and gave it vitality, producing what we call our 'energy', life in nature, the movement of water and the growth of plants. In order to exist, they concluded, everything required the 'breath of life'.

But the very fact that mankind does not enjoy constantly idyllic existence demonstrated to the ancient Chinese that the *Chi* could not always be flowing smoothly. Clearly its progress was sometimes interrupted, resulting in bad Feng Shui. This stagnant *Chi* they named *Sha* and set about finding countermeasures to ensure a smooth flow. The worst causes of bad Feng Shui, they discovered, were straight lines, sharp corners, dead ends—shapes that prevented the *Chi* from circulating around any given spot, especially a home or garden. By altering these 'obstructions'—sometimes in the simplest ways, such as deflecting it with curved surfaces or mirrors, for example—the 'breath of life' could be assured a smooth passage. (As a matter of interest, according to the acupuncturists there are four types of the 'breath of life' circulating in the body: 'Guarding', 'Internal Organ', 'Original' and 'Protein', and at the moment of death the *Chi* departs from the body.)

The scholars of Feng Shui took careful note of the evidence all around them pointing to a constantly changing universe. This, they decided, must be caused by the interaction of two continually moving forces, which they envisaged as light and dark, active and passive, positive and negative, male and female. They named these forces *Yin* for the darker, negative, female side, and *Yang* for the brighter, active, male side. These they saw not simply as opposites, but rather as the harmonious balance of two forces in which one could not exist without the other, and which in conjunction with the *Chi* pervaded all things, living and organic, generating harmony and good health.

The symbol which the Chinese devised to represent *Yin* and *Yang* is shown in the illustration opposite. To clarify the relationship between it and the other elements, let us turn to one of the earliest and still most comprehensive summaries of the concept in English, written by Thomas Taylor Meadows (1819–69), a consular official in Canton for many years and a widely respected scholar on early Chinese history. He wrote of this philosophy in his work, *The Chinese and Their Rebellions* (1862):

All nature, animate and inanimate—the Universe in the widest or proper sense of the word—is based on, and subsists by an ultimate Entity, the specific or proper name of which is Tai Chi. This term rendered literally means the Grand Extreme; and it is intended to express the extreme point to which man's speculations on the nature of existence have been able to reach. As this Grand Extreme, which I have just called an Entity, is absolutely immaterial and as it operates in the process by which the material universe is produced in an invariable way, yet without intelligence and without will, it may be viewed as a Law—as the fixed Order in which all the multifold and varied phenomena of the Universe take place. I shall therefore call the Tai Chi the Ultimate Principle.

The Ultimate Principle has operated from eternity, and now ceaselessly works, by a dynamical process in virtue of which animate and inanimate nature has

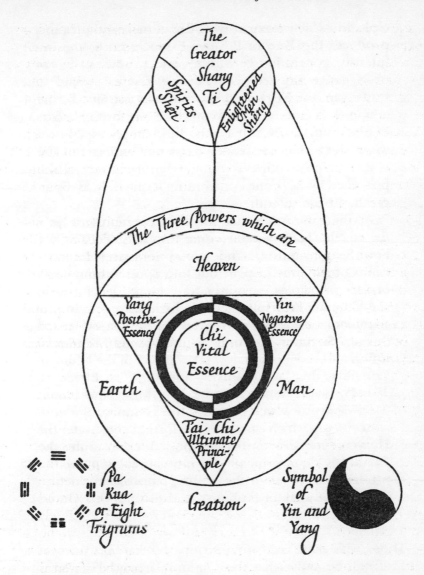

The vital elements of Feng Shui. From an old diagram.

existed from all eternity. This process is represented as pulsative, as a succession of active-expansive, and passive-intensive states; which succession, as already indicated, never had a beginning. The Ultimate Principle, in its 'active-expansive' operation, constitutes and produces the *Yang* or Positive Essence; in its 'passive-intensive' operation constitutes and produces the *Yin* or Negative Essence. The Positive Essence is said to transform, the Negative Essence is said to unite. By the action thus indicated they produce the five elements of the material world: earth, fire, water, metal and wood. By which the reader must not understand the visible, palpable things so named, but five essences, one possessed by each, and constituting it what it is, as distinguished from the others.

At the same time that the Five Elements are produced, the Four Seasons come into existence. By the Four Seasons must be understood not merely four divisions of the time of year, but four special though secondary principles, or rather four specialised forms of the Ultimate Principle each of which has a certain predominance in nature during one of the periods called Spring, Summer, Autumn, Winter. A transcendental union and coagulation now takes place, of the Ultimate Principle, the Two Essences, and the Five Elements. The Positive Essence becomes the Masculine Power, the Negative Essence becomes the Feminine Power— conceived in which character the former constitutes the Heavenly mode or principle, the latter constitutes the Earthly mode or principle. By mutual reaction, the two produce all things in the visible, palpable world; and the double work of evolution and dissolution goes on without end.

Those who have read my previous book, *The Way of Feng Shui*, will be aware that the *Chi* and *Yin* and *Yang* are just the first of a number of factors that enable them to use Feng Shui to set right their home or, in the case of those early Chinese, find the correct spot on which to raise a shrine, site a temple, or even dig a grave. Among the items most frequently used in this branch of Feng Shui are a compass known as the *Luopan*, which has a number of complex bands of symbols and characters to help the *xiansheng* discover a suitable site; a series of eight trigrams collectively called the *bagua*, which consists of three broken and/or solid lines in various combinations and is a remarkable repository of knowledge that has been explained in the famous textbook, the *I Ching*; and the unique square of nine numbers known as the *Lo Shu*, in which every row of figures, horizontal, diagonal, and vertical, adds up to the same number, 15, and can be used to predict the future. Their role is less crucial in the garden, but the reader who wishes to know more about them should consult *The Way of Feng Shui*.

However, the ideas embodied in *Yin* and *Yang* are very important in Feng Shui gardening if one wishes to create the right balance between the house and garden and, in turn, the trees, plants and flowers and structural features. As I have already indicated, paths linking the house and garden should be curved or zigzagged (but never twisted as this can 'tie up' the *Chi*), and stone or pebble mosaics, whether on a path or a patio, will help to emphasise the duality of *Yin* and *Yang*. If you decide to have a small bridge somewhere in the garden, such as over a stream or pool, this should be arched.

Brick walls and wooden screens which link house and garden are also recommended. Feng Shui suggests making an opening in them as this symbolises the difference between heaven and earth and also adheres to the *Yin/Yang* principles. Known as the *hau chi'ang* or ornamental walls, they come in two types: those with an opening made in a fantastic shape through which the world beyond can be seen, or those which reveal a carefully prepared landscape to give the impression of greater space. A small pavilion (or summerhouse) with round and square windows can have the same effect of helping the passage of the 'breath of life'.

Statues of symbolic animals, which the Chinese have used for centuries, are also good for the *Chi*: such renowned Feng Shui creatures as the dragon and tortoise can help both the natural energy and the dual forces. In the next chapter I shall be explaining how the four sides of the garden are

A hole in a garden wall providing a panoramic view, especially of water, is good Feng Shui. These openings are known as *hau chi'ang*.

each associated with a famous creature of Chinese legend and how they are used in planning a garden to conform to the guidelines of Feng Shui.

There is, however, another group of symbols which are just as important to the Feng Shui of a garden. These, referred to by Thomas Taylor Meadows, are known as the 'Theory of the Five Elements' or, more generally, the 'Five Energies'. They consist of Earth, Fire, Water, Metal and Wood.

According to the legendary Chinese sage Wu Hsing, who is said to have defined this particular aspect of Feng Shui philosophy around the third century BC, forces of energy move in five fundamental ways: *outwards* and *inwards*, *upwards* and *downwards*, and in *rotation*. Wu Hsing and his fellow scholars linked this concept to the elements of Wood, Fire, Metal and Water, with Earth as their centre point. The result

THE FIVE ENERGIES

ELEMENT	WOOD *(Outward)*	FIRE *(upward)*	EARTH *(rotation)*	METAL *(inward)*	WATER *(downward)*
PLANET	Jupiter	Mars	Saturn	Venus	Mercury
SEASON	spring	summer	transition	autumn	winter
DIRECTION	east	south	centre	west	north
WEATHER	wind	heat	sunshine	cold	rain
CLIMATE	blustery	hot	humid	dry	freezing
COLOUR	green	red	yellow	white	blue
SMELL	rancid	burnt	fragrant	rotten	putrid
TASTE	sour	bitter	sweet	pungent	salty

was essentially a study of the movement of energy, and it is one that has long played an important role in Feng Shui, especially where gardening is concerned, because of what it reveals about the vitality of our environment.

As the table of 'The Five Energies' shows, each movement of energy is expressed as a natural element which symbolises all the other energies of the same type. These energies are also associated with a number of familiar forces and senses, including the major planets of our solar system, the seasons of the year, the compass directions and even tastes and smells.

All these energies interact with one another in cyclical patterns which are at their most evident in the changing seasons of the year. As any gardener is aware, energy expands *outwards* in the spring, followed by the *upward* surge in the summer. Then, in the autumn, this energy begins to turn *inwards* and is followed by the *downward* spiral of winter. With the return of spring, the whole cycle of expanding, rising and condensing begins once more, driven by the rotating power of the Earth. Feng Shui explains the energy behind each symbol in this way:

- **WOOD** (Mu). The tree represents a great force of energy that can expand in all directions. It is symbolic of the beginning of a cycle of growth and the arrival of spring.
- **FIRE** (Huo). Flames shooting upwards are symbolic of this energy, which rises to a peak in the summer and then begins to diminish and decline.
- **EARTH** (Tu). The centre point of the five elements, where the energy rotates around its own axis, influencing the changing seasons. Here Earth is shown as a phase between the rise of Fire and the inward movement of Metal, but in some Feng Shui charts is pictured as the centre point around which the other four energies revolve.
- **METAL** (Chin). This power condenses as it moves inwards during the autumn, making it the most concentrated of the energies and symbolic of the coagulat-

ing of energy that occurs before the onset of winter.
- **WATER** (Shui). Symbolic of energy descending towards a period of rest and stillness in the depths far from the light, during the inhospitable conditions of winter.

The early exponents of Feng Shui also established how the five energies interacted with one another in what they referred to as the 'Creative Cycle' and the converse 'Control Cycle'. With these formulae they were able to demonstrate how the five energies can be used to harness the influence and intensity of each other.

Creative Cycle
WOOD
burns creating
FIRE
which leaves
EARTH
from which comes
METAL
that flows like
WATER
which grows
WOOD
and so on

Control Cycle
FIRE
will melt
METAL
that cuts down
WOOD
which draws goodness from
EARTH
that pollutes
WATER
which quenches
FIRE
and so on

In gardening terms, Feng Shui says the Five Energies can be used to ensure that the various elements of a garden are in harmony with one another—factors such as the shape and colour of any construction in the ground—so that the *Chi* will have a smooth passage and be able to affect the well-being of everyone who walks there. Many people, of course, have an intuitive feel for shape and colour, and such instincts should not be ignored when planning a garden. The shapes themselves will naturally affect the flow of energy in and around them. The main points that Feng Shui makes can be summarised as follows:

- **WOOD**. As symbolic of expansion and growth, it is represented by buildings that are rectangular in shape. The energy inherent in wood is best shown by shades of green.
- **FIRE**. The upward rush of flames suggests triangular-shaped buildings or those with pointed roofs. This powerful energy lends itself to the colour red.
- **EARTH**. The most commonplace shape of all, a square, is symbolic of the stability and security of earth. Such buildings have either gently-sloping or flat roofs, and should be decorated in either yellow or brown.
- **METAL**. Circular or round buildings are symbolic of metal where the energy is concentrated inwards. Like metal itself, such structures should be painted white.
- **WATER**. Buildings that undulate or have indented roofs resembling flowing water are symbolic of Water energy. The best colour for them is, naturally, blue.

In the very early days of Feng Shui, the sages exploring its applications realised that it was important to protect a house and its lands from harmful *Sha* invading from the outside. One way to counter such forces was to put up a 'protective' element close by, such as a tree, a hedge, even a small wall. Then, with further experimentation, they learned that they could enhance 'the lifeblood of the living earth' (as the *Chi* is occasionally described in mystical circles) by creating gardens in previously barren areas around their homes, and by including features like paths, ponds, rock gardens and small pavilions along with flowers, plants and trees of special symbolic significance.

Indeed, it became obvious to these pioneers that what they had done in a house to improve its Feng Shui—changing the colour scheme of a room, realigning the furnishings or introducing a mirror—could be achieved just as effectively out of doors. There was very little difference in this concept, it seemed, from a gardener moving a plant closer to, or farther away from, the sunlight in order to improve its growth. Position and orientation were all-important, and the *Chi* could be harnessed just as successfully in the garden as in the house.

The very earliest Feng Shui manual to mention gardening, the *Yuan Ze*, says that the best kind of garden is created when there are rough textures contrasting with smooth—as in stationary rocks balanced by running water, for example. Because of this, the Chinese believed that the perfect site for a garden would be by the side of a lake with a view of mountains. Today there are such gardens to be found in China, Japan, Hong Kong, Singapore and even in a few countries farther west, but such a location is obviously impossible for most of us. So the principles of Feng Shui have to be adapted on a smaller scale where, experience has shown, they will function equally well to put man and nature in harmony and balance.

In creating a Feng Shui garden it is important to realise that the interaction of the Five Elements is crucial to the harmony, especially where there may be outside influences that could threaten its *Chi*. In order to set up counter-measures, you need first to establish the orientation of your property and then introduce a controlling element. Let us just remind ourselves of the directions associated with each of the elements:

NORTH: Water
SOUTH: Fire
EAST: Wood
WEST: Metal
CENTRE: Earth

Next we must consult the Feng Shui table designed to show the appropriate controlling elements for any threatening feature. It was first drawn up centuries ago as a guide to the symbolism of mountains of different shapes—an *indented* mountain represents Water, a *peaked* mountain Fire, a *rounded* mountain, Wood, a *curved* mountain Metal and a *square* mountain Earth—but here it has been adapted to cover the kind of structures most likely to occur in a modern Western community.

GARDEN ORIENTATION	
Threatening Element	Counter-Element
FIRE (spires, towers)	WATER (pond, fountain)
WOOD (poles, trees)	METAL (sculpture, frames)
EARTH (mounds, huts)	WOOD (plants, summer-house)
METAL (iron structures)	FIRE (red flowers)
WATER (wires, pylons)	EARTH (garden ornaments)

Once you have established the direction in which your garden faces, and the element associated with it, then the table can be used to set up a barrier against any threatening element in the street or on adjoining land. To illustrate what I mean, if there is a feature classified as **METAL** overlooking a garden which faces in a **WOOD** direction, there is a danger of the *Chi* 'wasting away' and the counter-element **WATER** should be introduced. In everyday terms: if there is a lamp-post or electricity pylon outside a house with a north-facing garden, this can harm the growth of plants and should be effectively controlled by building a small ornamental pond (**WATER**) or by growing a bed of red flowers (**FIRE**).

It may happen, of course, that a garden facing south is overlooked by such structures, but as the matching elements do not clash with one another, no countermeasures are necessary. Only if a lamp-post or pylon were directly aligned with the front door would a countermeasure be required in the form of a curved path to the doorway, in order to encourage the smooth flow of *Chi* into the house and garden.

However, now that you have secured your property against outside interference, we come to the more exciting and fulfilling business of planning and actually laying out a Feng Shui garden. Here again, the ideas are based upon the very oldest traditions, but can be adapted and successfully put into effect anywhere today.

3 *PLANNING A FENG SHUI GARDEN*

Two famous creatures of Chinese mythology play an important role in 'mapping out' a garden to utilise its powers and benefits. This pair, the dragon and the phoenix, are part of a group known as the 'Five Animals', which is completed by the tiger, the tortoise and the snake. Each has its own symbolism and application to a different area of the garden.

The Chinese believe that buildings which face south have the best Feng Shui because it symbolises warmth and goodness, and the same is naturally true of gardens. Therefore we find that four of the Five Animals have each been assigned to a general point of the compass with the fifth, the snake, forming the central point. Feng Shui summarises their symbolism and the directions with which they are associated as follows:

DRAGON East (*Wen*)
Colour: **Azure**
Element: **Wood**
According to the oldest Oriental traditions, the dragon is the figure of spring. It is never visible in our world and is believed to remain just out of sight above the clouds where

it observes everything and takes note of what is going on below. The creature represents foresight and stability and is also symbolic of human wisdom at its most spiritual. The characteristics of the dragon are protection, benevolence, culture, civility and good fortune. (Feng Shui says that the dragon should always be on the left-hand side of anything, and to this day, many Chinese refer to their left side as the 'dragon side'.)

PHOENIX South (*Feng Huang*)
Colour: **Red**
Element: **Fire**
The phoenix is the bird of ancient myth which is said never to die. It is associated with summer and has the ability to see into the future. It is also the provider of information about the surrounding area as well as a bringer of good luck. The characteristics associated with this beautiful bird are happiness, hope, joy, fame and fortune. Legend says that the phoenix perches in the famous *Wutung* tree (the Chinese parasol tree, *Firmiana simplex*), which is one reason why this ornamental tree with its edible seeds—eaten in moon cakes at the autumn festival—is a great favourite in many Chinese gardens. (In very old Feng Shui charts the phoenix is sometimes represented as a peacock, pheasant or cockerel.)

TIGER West (*Wu*)
Colour: **White**
Element: **Metal**
The magnificent white tiger is the animal of autumn and stands for strength. It is said to be constantly on the alert for danger from outside, and has the power to attack as well as defend. According to some authorities, although the animal is essential for survival, it also serves as a personal warning of the violence which can lie dormant within us all. The characteristics of the tiger are power, anger, danger, speed and unpredictability.

TORTOISE North (*Yuan Wu*)
Colour: **Black**
Element: **Water**

Although portrayed as the creature of Winter, the tortoise, with its thick shell and impression of great self-sufficiency, is said to represent security and its position is always to the rear of the other animals. Because of its shell, it symbolises protection against attack for all those who live on a property. The characteristics of the tortoise are caring, nurturing, mystery, hidden depths and sleep. (The tortoise is sometimes replaced in Feng Shui symbolism by a giant turtle.)

SNAKE Centre (*Jung*)
Colour: **Brown**
Element: **Earth**

The snake is not aligned on any compass point, but holds the vital position of central pivot around which the other creatures and the seasons turn. Coloured like the earth on which it lives, the snake lies coiled and ever alert, ready to receive information gathered by the dragon, phoenix, tiger and tortoise. This it uses to take any action necessary to preserve the harmony of the environment. The characteristics of the snake are stability, patience, action, forcefulness and wisdom.

These, then, are the first considerations which Feng Shui says should be applied to any garden to ensure that it circulates the necessary *Chi* around the property to engender well-being for the residents and flourishing vegetation.

In days gone by a house in China could be sited just about anywhere, which meant that a south-facing position was always perfectly feasible. In the modern Western world, however—especially in towns and cities—it is much harder to find a property with such an orientation. But do not despair, because Feng Shui believes that so long as each side of a garden is allocated its correct 'animal' side, the flow of the vital *Chi* can be assured everywhere. To help you work this out, here is the advice given by Jiang Ping Jie, a Feng Shui *xiansheng* and a keen gardener, who lives in Singapore:

Finding out which is your tortoise side of the garden is vital, and in fact whether it turns out to be in the front or back garden depends on the walls of your home. The phoenix aspect will always be at the end farthest away from the house [whether or not this is the southern end]. So if you look at the Feng Shui plan of the Five Animals [reproduced here] you'll see that the back wall of the house faces the larger part of the garden at the rear. So in this case, that rear wall is the tortoise side of both the house and the garden.

Now let us imagine a property with all the animal sides established, and consider the other requirements necessary to fulfil the rules of Feng Shui.

Obviously, if the house *does* face south, the phoenix aspect will be in the ideal position to promise good fortune. Accord-

The Feng Shui positions of the 'Five Animals' in a garden.

ing to Jiang Ping Jie, some Chinese are even more fussy when choosing a house and look for a property that faces exactly south-east. They believe that such a place will guarantee them not only the luck of the mythical red bird, but also the protection of the dragon stationed on the eastern flank.

There are two important factors to bear in mind about the land between the house and the farthest point of the garden. Feng Shui says it should not slope down steeply as this might make it difficult for the phoenix to maintain its position; nor should it be too flat as this could cause the good *Chi* to stagnate. A gently sloping incline is ideal. As a general rule, in order to create a sense of openness and ensure a pleasant view, the phoenix aspect of the garden should not be densely planted. Small shrubs are best put here and, if you fancy growing one, a herb garden (see chapter 9).

The sun, of course, rises on the dragon side if it faces east. Because of this, Feng Shui lore maintains that it is a good energy centre and an ideal location in which to plant trees or tall bushes that are symbolic of strength and protection. Trees like the pine and willow are very popular with the Chinese for this part of a garden because they are said to promote long life (I shall explain all about the energy of trees in chapter 6). Some Chinese gardeners make a point of forming an L-shaped corner of trees linking the dragon aspect to that of the phoenix, in order to enhance the Feng Shui of the whole area. It is also recommended that the highest point of a garden should be on the dragon side— a point to be borne in mind by anyone considering landscaping their property.

The tiger patrols the right-hand side of a garden, and this is best kept as a flat, low-lying area. By doing this a gardener can follow the Feng Shui guidelines to avoid any hills or mountains to the west of a building, as these may harbour ill-fortune. A steep slope could also disturb the property's composure. This is the area of the garden best suited to the growing of low shrubs and flowers, and the correct combi-

nation of such plants will generate enough *Chi* to ensure
the harmony of the whole area. I shall be discussing the
most suitable varieties in chapter 5.

FIVE ANIMALS PLANTING GUIDE	
PHOENIX	shrubs, herb bed
DRAGON	trees, large bushes
TIGER	flowers, low shrubs
TORTOISE	small evergreens, border plants
SNAKE	lawn, small hardy annuals

The location of the fourth aspect, the tortoise side, has
already been explained by Jiang Ping Jie. He told me that
any gardener who wants to strengthen the tortoise elements
of safety and protection around a building should adapt the
old Feng Shui idea of siting a house near hills to provide it
with protection from the cold north winds. To achieve this,
the level of the ground near the rear wall should be raised
slightly, and the best things to grow here are small evergreen
and border plants.

Finally, there is the snake in the centre of the garden.
This area should contain a minimum of vegetation and is
best left as grass in an oval or circular shape. Meandering
gravel paths or paving stones can also be laid here to help the
Chi circulate readily. Never be tempted into making straight
paths as these are conductors of *Sha* and act like arrows to
disturb the harmony of the garden. The best kind of plants
for this area are small hardy annuals.

Feng Shui believes that paved areas should be designed
to facilitate peace, rest and contemplation, and built neither
too close to, nor too far from, the house. Too close and
there is the likelihood of being distracted by things like the
telephone; too far and there is the tedious business of trek-
king to and from the house for anything you might need.
If the only place for a paved area is close to the house or
flat, it should be screened or trellised with suitable plants
like climbing roses or wisteria to make it as separate and

idyllic a little hideaway as possible. As with everything concerning Feng Shui, finding the right balance is paramount.

When paving-stones, blocks of granite or even old York stone flags are used for such an area, allow a little space between them. Feng Shui says that a pattern in the *bagua* shape (or a herringbone if you prefer) is a good conductor of *Chi*, and the effect can be reinforced by inserting some compact or mat-forming plants in the cracks. These will also help divert any bad *Sha*. An expert told me that any members of the dianthus family like pinks are good for this purpose, as well as aromatic thyme which, of course, will tolerate being walked over and trodden upon. It is also a good idea in large paved areas to leave a number of irregular small holes here and there filled with good, rich soil in which compact little shrubs with good Feng Shui can be planted to improve both the appearance and the *Chi*. Mound-forming plants grown in such terraces can look very effective when they have matured and spilled over to soften the edges of the surrounding slabs.

Of course no two gardens are ever completely alike, and the very last thing Feng Shui advocates is trying to make them all the same. Variety and personal taste are strongly encouraged, although always with the proviso that hard corners and straight lines should be avoided. Apart from encouraging the flow of the energies, a garden must be harmonious and attractive to its owners, and for centuries the Chinese have maintained that particular shapes have powers of their own which can be very influential.

There should always be a clear distinction between the house and garden, no matter how small either may be. The perfect shape for a house is a complete rectangle, so it is important to bear in mind that if you add an extension, extra rooms or a conservatory, you should try to ensure that they extend right along one side of the rectangle to preserve its shape. If there is such an addition there already, or you have no option but to leave a vacant space which creates a sharp corner or L-shape, then introduce into this area some anti-*Sha* items like pot plants, a statue or a small tree, or perhaps even a little fountain. Ornamental features have always been popular with the Chinese, although style and scale in relation to their surroundings are major factors when selecting urns, planters and pots, as well as what is grown in them. A few simple, well-designed pots of stone or simulated stone, filled with a single species of plant, can enhance the whole garden, and are far better than a lot of huge urns stuffed with multicoloured plants. Feng Shui *hates* ostentation, for as the old Chinese saying goes, 'Ornament has no defined order; if it provides distraction, that is sufficient.'

Where a garden is rectangular in shape, gardeners should not divide the plot up into regimented beds and borders, nor try to fill every part of it. Make the most of open space to create a natural vista in which flowers, plants and trees are all in balance with one another. In the case of an irregularly shaped plot, the main area of garden should be on the dragon side of the house, taking care to avoid doing anything by way of cultivation that could weaken the tortoise's role and make the house vulnerable to the attacks of bad *Sha*. End-of-street houses, which quite often seem to be situated on a triangular-shaped piece of land, will have to maintain Feng Shui principles by creating two quite separate gardens—one perhaps put down to lawn with shrubs, and the other concentrating on flowerbeds.

The vast majority of gardens in towns, cities and suburbs, however, tend to be narrow and of differing lengths. In fact they lend themselves admirably to Feng Shui, and by astute use of plants and ornaments it is possible to disguise the size and shape and give the impression that you have built a little oasis of naturalness in the heart of commuter-land. The use of discreetly placed outdoor-grade mirrors to reflect back intriguing views will not only make a garden seem larger and more inviting, but the mirror is, of course, one of the most effective weapons in the armoury of Feng Shui.

Another unusual feature that can be effectively created in a narrow garden is an octagonal area of stone and plants based on the Feng Shui *bagua* (see p. 48). The segments of this can, for example, be represented by an outer concentric

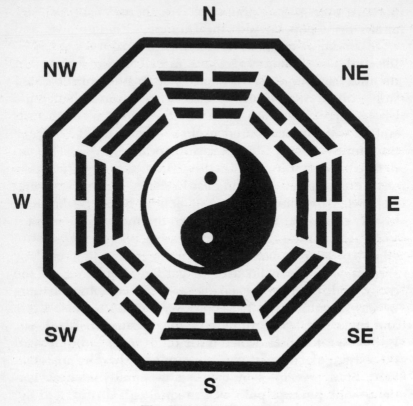

The Feng Shui *bagua.*

bed filled with a single variety of a low-growing evergreen plant. Next, a ring of stone blocks or bricks set into the soil in patterns. And, finally, in the middle, an equal division of two flowers of strongly contrasting colours symbolises *Yin* and *Yang.* This octagon, combining rocks and flowers, can really enhance the Feng Shui of a garden—but be warned that you *must* ensure when you lay it out that each piece of the pattern is facing in the correct compass direction or you will totally confuse the *Chi* and turn it into *Sha.* As another tip, you could introduce a weeping tree at the corner of the dragon/phoenix side, with an array of camellias in the middle of the phoenix aspect. The flowers will give you an additional *Yin/Yang* element which is especially noticeable in the spring when they produce their showy blooms to herald the bright days that lie ahead.

Feng Shui believes that hedges can also play an important role in the garden, but it frowns on topiary as this deprives trees and shrubs of their natural shape. Bushes with wide, dark green leaves are the best conductors of *Chi* and they should never be forced to grow in straight lines or be clipped too formally, but allowed to develop a natural look. A hedge can create a sense of intimacy, and when grown along a curving pathway can lead to unexpected visual delights and fragrances in other parts of the garden. The importance of the smell of flowers in Feng Shui is another factor that should never be underestimated, because the Chinese believe that the 'breath of life' circulates even more smoothly when carried along by enchanting perfumes.

As well as making sure that your paths meander, you should also take account of their direction. Those from a westerly point should wind as much as possible, while those from the south can curve more gently because the Chinese say the most invigorating *Chi* emanates from the south. However, Jiang Ping Jie once had a client who lived in a north-facing house with a path to the rear which brought the energy from the south. Because the path was too straight, it carried the *Chi* directly through the building and left all the occupants generally lacking in vitality. This all changed when the *xiansheng* introduced some curves to the path, along with a bamboo screen.

Screens are, in fact, very useful alongside paths or for masking unsightly boundary walls or fences. Similarly, trellis panels and pergola tunnels, over which flowering and fruiting plants can be trained, are good Feng Shui. (Pergolas, with their ability to alter our perception of a garden's size and provide an enchanting experience as the whole environment momentarily changes, are also said to be useful for providing a balance between garden and house.) All such walkways are believed to be representative of long life, especially if bamboo is used in their construction. The bamboo has, of course, been associated with the Chinese since time immemorial, and certain species are now easy to grow in the West, which makes their use in the garden all the easier. For those who would like to try them I have included a chapter about the strength and special qualities of the bamboo.

If you prefer a conventional wall, an undulating line of mellow-coloured bricks should suffice very nicely, so long as your neighbours agree. Such walls leading in the direction of the house are said to attract wealth. I have already mentioned the value of openings in walls like the *hau ch'iang*, and it is also important in Feng Shui that where there is a wall around a house it is in proportion to the height and width of the building.

Water, as one of the fundamental elements in Feng Shui, has a special place in the garden. The streams which flowed across the Chinese landscape were seen as symbolic of bringing wealth, and when they were introduced into gardens they were normally diverted in from the east to assist the flow of the *Chi*. This still holds good today, although any man-made watercourse such as a stream or a pond is permissible at the southern end. It is important that any pond you build should have a natural shape and not be made square or rectangular. The water should also be surrounded by appropriate flowers and if it is stocked with goldfish they will attract good luck. Whatever else, a peaceful stretch of water reflecting the surrounding scenery, or with goldfish darting below the surface suggesting another dimension, is the very epitome of balance and harmony.

The original rock gardens in China were just that—small-scale reproductions of the mountain ranges that people saw all around them, which provided protection to those who dwelt in their shadow. These 'miniature landscapes' are said to be representative of continuity, and ideally should be placed to the north of any stretch of water in a garden. These two features should be as close together as possible because of their *Yin* and *Yang* qualities. A rockery represents hills which are the source of life because they provide mankind with water. Hence they are regarded as *Yang*. The pond, with its water, is a *Yin* feature and provides the necessary

The curled roof edges of this Chinese house encourage good
Feng Shui for the building and its garden.

harmony. If there is not enough room in your garden for
both a pond and a rockery, you could create a small island
in the middle of the pond and place a suitable *Yang* element
upon it, such as a tiny gazebo, model pavilion or a typical
Chinese pagoda. I shall be returning to the subject of rockeries and ponds in chapter 8.

  The summer-house, which has become such a familiar
sight in many Western gardens, is actually only a modern
version of the old Chinese garden pavilions which are to be
seen in countless old artists' prints and engravings. These
and the elegant pagodas which once adorned the country's
landscape were deliberately placed in the north-east or
south-west corners of gardens to repel the evil influences
which folk tradition said came from the 'Doors of the Devil'.
Today, they stand there to repel bad *Sha*. The number of
sides a pavilion (or pagoda) may have is also of significance
in Feng Shui. A square-shaped building is symbolic of the
stability of earth, while one with five sides is linked to the
benefits of the Five Elements. Those with six sides are rep-

resentative of wealth, and those with eight sides are an indicator of prosperity.

Here, finally, are two tips if you happen to live in a very angular house which is interfering with the *Chi* you are so painstakingly trying to cultivate in the garden. One way to soften the hard edges is to allow a climbing plant such as a wisteria or clematis to grow up the walls. Many gardeners cherish the notion that a cluster of roses growing up the side of a house is as English as the country cottage, but in fact the Chinese were doing just this for hundreds of years before the birth of Christ. They also learned that it is important to allow the 'breath of life' to pass over the roofs of their houses, which is why many Chinese buildings have edges that curl up at the corners, sometimes in the most elaborate designs. My second tip—if you don't want to go to such lengths—is that the same beneficial effect can be achieved by hanging wind chimes at the corners of the building. I have certainly seen any number of these in Chinese communities as far apart as Singapore, Australia and the West Coast of America. I assume they were working because everyone looked so happy and full of energy.

If there is a secret to making a successful Feng Shui garden, it may be found in the words of the scholarly monk Tao Chi, a painter and writer who lived during the time of the Ming dynasty, between the fourteenth and seventeenth centuries. This man, who delighted in his love of horticulture by calling himself the 'Monk of the Bitter Cucumber', wrote about and sketched a number of ornate gardens which had quite evidently been created along Feng Shui lines. 'The vital forces of the landscape,' he said, 'should be expressed by making some parts in them wide open and other parts hidden or screened.' It is a piece of advice, I suggest, always to have in mind when planning your own version.

4 *PUTTING ON A GOOD FRONT*

It is a curious fact that many people spend a great deal of time working on their back gardens and virtually ignore the front. Of course a lot of suburban front gardens are very small, but surely even the smallest of them deserves better than being just somewhere to park the car or stand the dustbins?

Many centuries ago the Chinese understood that the front garden of a house reflected the personality of those who lived inside. Feng Shui went farther and said that the front entrance to any building was actually its 'mouth' and the point at which the life-enhancing *Chi* entered. Hence the situation of this door was very important—as were the surrounding features in the garden—in order that the flow of the earth's energies might be unimpeded.

According to Feng Shui, the free movement of the *Chi* in the front garden not only benefits the residents, but creates an 'aura' which reveals quite a lot about the inhabitants. Some readers will immediately quote the old adage, 'Never judge a book by its cover', but the fact is we *do*, and a house is frequently judged by its frontage.

I have also heard it said that front gardens are everybody's little patch of ostentation, but even so they should relate not only to the style of the house itself, but to the whole street as well. Feng Shui offered ground rules to achieve this long before gardening as we know it had made its impact on the West. Indeed, the ancient art had already said very much what Humphrey Repton, one of the great English landscape designers, wrote in the eighteenth century—that all gardens should have 'unity, utility and proportion'. In a nutshell, this implies that a front garden should have a consistent theme, the various elements should be in scale with one another and, perhaps most important of all, it should be fit for its purpose. To keep such an area *simple* should be the byword, whether the site is extensive or just a few precious feet.

No matter if a garden is in a city, town or village, with the help of Feng Shui even the most modest strip can be turned into a plot that is varied, attractive and beneficial. It can also make more of a statement about you and your home than the colours of your walls, doors and windows. Indeed, because of their differing sizes, all gardens represent a challenge to both the experienced gardener and the novice to experiment with the layout and planting. Many of the lessons learnt on a small scale at the front of a property can then be repeated with more confidence at the rear.

As the front garden is not where people generally linger, Feng Shui says it should be used to make a bold impact and compete with the activity of the road. Ideally, too, it should act as a screen for the house. There is no point in going in for too much detail or using subtle plants here—that is something for the rear where everyone can relax and enjoy them.

The first feature to tackle in the front garden is without question the path to the front door. On many Western properties there is a tendency for drives and paths to be laid in straight lines from the road to the door. This is not ideal as the straightness will hurry the *Chi* into the house and, if the back door is aligned to the front, as is often the case, will cause it to leave at the rear just as quickly. A path that narrows as it nears the front door will act as a funnel and

The front garden of a house is all-important, according to Feng Shui. Note the position of the tree to deflect bad *Sha* from the entranceway.

concentrate the *Chi* too much, while one that widens can only dissipate the energy flow.

There is a charming description by an eighteenth-century French visitor to China, Père Attivet, which sums up the thinking behind Feng Shui pathways. 'What is strange is that they never go in a straight line,' he says. 'They make a hundred detours, sometimes behind a clump of bushes, sometimes behind a rock, or sometimes round a lake; there is nothing so agreeable. In all this there is an enchanting, elevating impression of the countryside.'

According to Feng Shui, the ideal front drive is almost horseshoe-shaped—as this sketch from a nineteenth-century traveller's notebook shows—entering the property from the south-east. Where this is not possible, the path should curve in from the road. If by chance it slopes down towards the front door, this is a very good omen, for it will help good luck and wealth flow into the home. If the opposite is the case, the process may be reversed by installing some posts at the steepest point to deflect the *Chi* into a beneficial curve. I have been told that a small garden light placed on such slopes can be equally effective.

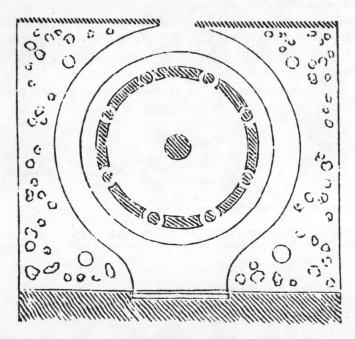

An ideal Feng Shui circular driveway from a nineteenth-century Western visitor's travel book, and (*opposite*) the same idea adapted for modern Western houses.

The whole effect of a path curving towards the front door will be to generate a sense of invitation, whereas driveways which run in straight lines or alongside a house can only cause the earth energies to by-pass it and create an unwelcoming impression. I feel sure that, like me, many readers will have experienced the sensation when entering certain buildings, regardless of age, of an inexplicable coldness and dampening of the spirits. The Chinese say this is caused by the absence of the *Chi.*

When choosing a raw material for your path—be it bricks, gravel, tarmacadam or concrete—making sure you pick one that blends in with the architectural style of the house as well as being durable and practical. In some gardens a narrow strip of soil alongside a winding path can be transformed into a delightful small avenue of plants which will aid the flow of the *Chi* if they are Feng Shui favourites such as roses or hydrangeas.

If you feel like being more adventurous, you could follow the Chinese preference for different-coloured pebbles, stone chips and even roof tiles turned on their edges to create all kinds of geometric patterns. Some even go as far as pictures in stone of lucky symbols such as birds, flowers and goldfish. In the back garden of the Imperial Palace in Peking there is a wonderfully meandering path which shows a number of

scenes from Chinese history and even a man on one of the nation's ubiquitous bicycles.

In some gardens, the path to the front door may have steps. So long as these are curved, and there are suitable elements to prevent the *Chi* running away, no harm is being done. However, many Western gardeners delight in putting rocks alongside such paths. Attractive as they may appear, this is bad Feng Shui because the rocks effectively block the 'mouth' of the house and prevent a regular flow of energy. It is much better to have a smooth patch of grass on either side of the steps. The Feng Shui of the steps themselves is also improved by putting matching containers of flowers at the top or bottom of the flight. The plants should all be of the same colour and can be changed with the seasons. Among the most highly recommended species are chrysanthemums and pinks.

Whether your front door has a porch or merely opens onto the path, avoid any unnecessary obstructions. Never clutter the 'mouth' with storage boxes, piles of logs or even dustbins as these will harm the flow of the *Chi.* Any plants close to a door should be rounded in shape (a clipped ball of box (*Buxus* sp.) is recommended) to counter the vertical lines of the building.

When selecting plants for the front garden, the general rule is quite unequivocally 'mix and match'—but concentrate on two or three colours and avoid a complicated planting scheme as this can easily make the whole area look too busy and contrived. The ancient Chinese knew the value of simplicity, and wherever they wanted any kind of special feature opted for small pots or pieces of sculpture.

Harmony is also the keynote when choosing the colours of the plants for your front garden, so that they do not clash with the colours of the house and generate bad *Sha.* One expert told me that the secret to achieving this harmony is to choose plants in exactly the same way as you would select fabrics and furnishings for a room indoors.

There is no doubt that plants grown in containers are ideal for a small front garden, and there is evidence that

centuries ago the Chinese were using the same kind of earthenware pots we see about the front of Western houses today.
Whole books have been written on the varied ways that containers and plants can be combined to enhance the look of
a garden, but a few pointers drawn from the experience
of a couple of Feng Shui gardeners should be enough to
encourage the reader to experiment.

The great advantage of containers in the small garden is
that they restrain the growth of the plants and prevent them
taking over the entire area. They can also be moved about
at will and the design of a garden can be changed almost
weekly if so desired. Always look at the garden from the
street and not just standing in it, for sometimes quite small
movements can have the most dramatic effects when seen
from the viewpoint of the passer-by.

It is important to consider the shape of the pots as much
as the colour and mix of the plants in them—not forgetting
the juxtaposition of them all so that a balanced effect is
achieved. Use plants of different heights and shapes, combined with a variety of pots—there is a lot of fun to be
had in seeking the best effect. You can bring a whole new
dimension to even the most unprepossessing piece of
ground. In city areas, I have to recommend that gardeners
go for the larger, heavier pots as these are less likely to be
stolen. Even then it may be necessary to secure them with
chains.

Ideal for the front garden are the glazed and unglazed
pots made in China and the Far East which are now widely
available in the West. They come in a range of shades, including dark blue, sepia and green, which combine well with
most colour schemes. It is a good idea when planning to
use a number of containers in this way to buy them all
together so that you can be sure of creating a unified scheme.

Evergreen plants are essential in any front garden, not
only because of their distinctive shapes and the fact that
they look good all year round, but also because the hardier
varieties are resistant to the traffic fumes which can be the
curse of any garden in a town or city. 'Weeping' trees are

good Feng Shui, and do not forget the ornamental bamboos (especially the striking black bamboo) which are held in special regard as I shall explain in chapter 7.

Another item to consider for the front garden is a bird bath or small fountain. A bird bath in particular can attract good luck *and* wildlife, while either may be used as a means of diverting the *Chi* from any awkward straight lines. I know of several instances where home-owners have been advised by experts to put these little water features in the middle of a straight path, widening the path to encircle it and thereby creating curves.

Some of the early Feng Shui gardeners favoured less formal front gardens, allowing the plants and trees to grow more freely. However, they always ensured that there was a clear, winding path to the house to allow the vital energy access. Duplicating such an effect may not be possible in the very smallest city gardens, but can perhaps be achieved in a larger suburban garden. The result can be a front garden that not only creates seclusion about the house, but has a sound-proofing effect, insulating the inhabitants from the noise of passing traffic. Such a spot can give the impression of a rural retreat and will attract wildlife, but to create one will require many years of work; great care must also be taken that the deliberately informal look is not allowed to impede the flow of the *Chi.*

A final thought. Where a front garden is so tiny that there is really only room for flowerpots, by interchanging these regularly through the seasons of the year the owner can have blooms and scents the envy of a garden many times the size, as well as luxuriating in the best earth energies. The same applies to the humble window box, too.

5 THE FRAGRANT POWER OF FLOWERS

Two hundred years ago, some of the earliest Western travellers to China returned with breathless accounts of what they described as 'a world full of wonderful flowers'. These people—in the main European missionaries and merchant traders who had ventured beyond the coastal ports—marvelled at the glorious displays of peonies, chrysanthemums, lilies, asters, magnolias, wisteria, camellias, hydrangeas, azaleas, passion-flowers and roses. What puzzled them was that the flowers were evidently being cultivated, but in what appeared to be a totally informal, almost haphazard style. 'The leading idea of Chinese gardens seems to be to epitomise nature,' wrote an astute French Jesuit priest in the seventeenth century, 'to represent her in her various moods with due sense of proportion. In their love of flowers and trees, the Chinese are lovers of beauty.'

It was to be a good many years before visitors such as these learned that the growing of flowers in China—the 'Flowery Land' as it became known—was very much subject to the rules of Feng Shui. What they did discover, however, was that while we in the West use the word 'garden' to describe pleasure grounds of all sorts, the Chinese differentiate. A *hua yuan* or flower garden, for example, must have a wall and is considered an important place; but a *hua p'u* is a place where flowers grow in clusters throughout the garden. (There is, incidentally, a vivid description of a Chinese flower garden in the novel *Hung Lou Meng*, which has been translated into English as *Dream of the Red Chamber*.)

The Chinese passion for flowers is not really surprising when one realises that it is one of the most flower-rich regions of the world. Since time immemorial the country has had an unequalled richness and diversity of flora that visiting botanists have successively and successfully transported all over the world. The reason for this wealth of plant life has been ascribed to a combination of unique geographical accidents. The mountain areas of China escaped the ravages of the great ice caps so that many species of plant were able to continue developing here while being wiped out in much of Europe and North America. Later, in the country's warm and temperate climate, three different types of flora—those of the sub-tropical south, the cold, drier north and the alpine species of the Himalayan foothills— all mingled and fused freely for thousands of years.

The great philosopher Confucius (551–479 BC) advocated that it was part of every man's duty to hold public office. However, many Chinese found this duty disagreeable or boring and so turned to Taoism which held precisely the opposite view. The result was a widespread reaction against state service and a movement among the aristocracy and intelligentsia towards creating gardens and growing flowers. They believed this would bring them into harmony with nature and protect them from the effects of evil and bad luck in their lives. Traditionally it was also considered necessary for a man of culture to know seven arts, one of which was the cultivation of flowers. In the Tao religion, one of the pleasures of Paradise is said to be the enjoyment of the companionship of the Eight Immortals. Each of these beings represents a trade and is designated by an emblem, a basket of flowers symbolising the gardener. These symbols are still to be found throughout Chinese art to the present day.

A nineteenth-century woodcut of a peony garden by Lin Ching.
Note the trellis-work at the rear and the use of rocks in the
flowerbeds.

Some of the very earliest flower gardens in China were
apparently made by warrior lords specifically to please
women, for their enjoyment while the men were away at war.
The most famous example of this is contained in the story
of the Emperor Genso who fell in love with a beautiful and
capricious young lady named Yokiki. His adoration was such
that no whim of hers was too outrageous for him to order
its instant fulfilment. For example, he arranged for the balcony of the royal palace, over which she leaned to admire
the flowers in the garden below, to be made from the rarest
fragrant woods; and he carpeted the stepping-stones
throughout this garden with lotus flowers so that her feet
never touched the ground. Tragically, however, one demand
too many drove the Emperor's servants beyond the point of

all reason, and they rebelled and killed Yokiki and brought about their master's downfall.

Long before Emperor Genso built his garden, Feng Shui had established that certain flowers have a mystical importance. The prunus blossom, for example, was said to be the emblem of spring; the lotus stood for summer and the chrysanthemum represented autumn. For a time, the lotus was declared to be the 'Flower of Flowers', but it was later displaced by the peony for reasons to which I shall come shortly. This lovely bloom in both its herbaceous and tree forms thereafter appeared in Chinese floral manuals such as the legendary *Mi Fu Hua Ching*, labelled the 'King of Flowers'.

According to Feng Shui, flowers have their own particular symbolisms. Plum blossom, for instance, represents beauty and youth, while bamboo stands for long life. All plants and trees can also be classified as either *Yin* or *Yang*. Those plants which are said to have the strongest *Yang* element are:

bamboo
cherry
chrysanthemum
orchid
peony
willow

While those with a powerful *Yin* element are:

apricot
jasmine
magnolia
pear
rhododendron
rose

Of perhaps even greater importance in the Feng Shui of flowers is their smell. The more fragrant the blossom the more power the flowers have to ensure harmony in the garden, and the greater their ability to enhance the lives of all those who come into contact with them. After years of study, the experts agreed that *Chi* flows best in the company of pleasant floral aromas, while those with an unpleasant smell only encourage the creation of *Sha*. Probably the earliest and still most widely consulted Chinese list of Feng Shui-approved native flowers and blossoms translates as follows:

honeysuckle
jasmine
lilac
lilies
lotus
pinks
roses
wisteria

Although for centuries much about China was enveloped in myth and legend, subsequent visits to the country by travellers from the West, coupled with the scholarly study of ancient Chinese books and documents about the history of its horticulture, have demonstrated what a paradise of flowers the country has long been. As the American explorer and plant collector J. F. Rock wrote in 1926, describing one Chinese province in the journal *The Horticulturist*: 'I have never in my life seen such magnificent scenery. If the writer of Genesis had seen the Tebbu country he would have made it the birthplace of Adam and Eve, for beside an endless variety of flowers there are even apple trees forty to fifty feet tall, but the apples are not the kind that would have tempted Eve.'

The English author Sir Osbert Sitwell, who travelled to China a decade later, wrote even more perceptively about the nation's attitude towards flowers in his *Penny Foolish* (1935). He appreciated that the Chinese attitude was very different from that of Europeans, and sensed that Feng Shui was at work—although he had no understanding of the ancient art to be able to put into words to explain his feelings:

The peonies, balancing gaily upon their special terraces, attain to a hitherto undreamed-of-perfection; especially the tree-peonies. In colour they range through every shade from lotus-pink to so deep a purple that it is known as black.The buds have been cut off here and there, and a *great art* [my italics] has inspired the whole of the growing of the tree, while the terraces enable the onlooker to view it from a thousand different angles; for that is part of the Chinese theory of gardening.

Thus a blossoming tree must be viewed from above, as well as from beneath and at the side, and for this purpose are constructed those miniature mountains of rock which, at times when the trees are not in flower, seem so meaningless. But who that has seen it can ever forget the flowering of a cherry tree, when viewed from this particular unusual altitude? For it reveals a vista of winged life at which, before, one could only guess from the deep murmur inhabiting it. From above, as the blossoms lie displayed in the sun, you can watch the going and coming, the endless journeying of the bees and the fluttering of the butterflies.

The cultivation of wisteria, too, has attained in China a degree of excellence unknown here, and the blossom is treated in various and original ways. Sometimes an old vine is hung through a lattice, so that each drooping head is framed in a square; sometimes a stout tree has its serpentine branches supported by props of wood which look as though they were fashioned of coral, or, again, it is encouraged to writhe over a shallow pool so that it may be mirrored the better. And in these pleasances are found to perfection the natural stones which, in a Chinese garden, often take the place of statues and such-like edifices.

One or two of the early Western travellers noticed the local tradition of planting certain flowers in gardens in memory of deceased relatives. The Chinese have revered their dead since time immemorial, and it was believed that the spirits of those who had passed over could be placated and prevented from disturbing the places where they had been happiest while alive—such as a garden—by a small display of their favourite plants or flowers.

Feng Shui, which had long played a significant role in the siting of graveyards and tombs, also dictated the positioning of flowers associated with the dead in the part of the garden which they had most enjoyed; this, it was believed, would ensure harmony for the entire area. The appearance and fragrance of the flowers served as an ever-present reminder of the departed, as well as ensuring the smooth flow of the *Chi*. In some parts of China, the flowers of such plants are still picked on the anniversary of the death of the deceased and a single bloom given to relatives in remembrance. All those who love their gardens and perhaps dream of finally being at peace there in familiar surroundings will find something very hopeful and appealing about this tradition.

From a statistical point of view, it is interesting to note that when John Reinhold Forster published his great work *Florula Sinensis* in 1771, he listed a mere 260 species of Chinese plants. Today the number is about twenty thousand—since the beginning of the century, for example, over 500 new species of Chinese rhododendron have been discovered and catalogued. Indeed, it is true to say that we owe many of our most popular flowers to cuttings which originated behind the fabled 'Bamboo Curtain'. The *Chrysanthemum sinensis*, for instance, which was the ancestor of all our chrysanthemums, did not reach Europe until as late as 1680 when it was first imported by the Dutch. And today there is hardly a garden without at least one variety or another.

Few Western gardens are without roses, either, and I found it something of a surprise to learn that this beautiful and popular flower, of which many of the finest species came from China, is actually not the favourite of the people there. For although the rose has always been held in great esteem,

Another of Lin Ching's woodcuts, showing the Sui Yuan gardens in Nanking. Note the extensive use of bamboo as a screen, and the weeping willows around the water feature.

it is accorded less importance than the peony, lotus, chrysanthemum or prunus blossoms.

It seems likely that the Chinese were cultivating roses in gardens as early as 2700 BC, long before the Minoan artists were fashioning them in gold or painting them on the walls of their Cretan palaces. Roses certainly flourished in the Imperial Palace gardens in Peking during the fourth and fifth centuries BC, and Confucius recorded that the Emperor's library contained almost 600 books on roses. There was also a considerable number of works about peonies, lotus, chrysanthemums and rhododendrons (azaleas): one particular book on chrysanthemums, written by a certain Liu Ming at the time when William the Conqueror was invading Britain, not only divided the flower into 35 varieties but also gave detailed instructions on how to cultivate and utilise the plant in all manner of ways, from decoration to medicinal and even culinary use.

Feng Shui regards the rose as an exceptional plant and a good conductor of the earth's energies. The dried petals of the flower are said to be a protection against evil spirits, and the ruling classes of China were the first to discover the value of perfuming themselves with attar of roses. It was not until the eighteenth century, however, that the China rose made its way west in the hands of traders from the East India Company, and the first to arrive in Britain were known as the China roses (*Rosa chinensis* and *Rosa chinensis semperflorens*) — Slater's Crimson China in 1792 and Parson's Pink China in 1793. Later came the 'tea roses', those aristocrats of the rose world—Hume's Blush Tea-scented China in 1809 and Parks' Yellow Tea-scented China in 1824. A library of books almost as large as that in the Imperial Palace has since been written about the importance of China roses in the evolution of our modern roses—thanks in no small degree to Napoleon's wife, the Empress Josephine, who was among the first to realise their potential and created a beautiful garden of roses at Malmaison, complete with meandering paths, trellis screens and pergolas, in an unconscious copy of Feng Shui.

Certain Feng Shui *xiansheng* maintain that yellow roses are the best conductors of *Chi*, although others are undoubtedly more shapely and fragrant. There is an interesting account by a group of early European visitors to Canton in the middle of the sixteenth century describing the astonishment they felt when entering the famous Fa Tee nurseries on the outskirts of the city. There the party saw hundreds of white, pink, red and yellow roses growing on trellises and bamboo fences, as well as in a variety of pots that were obviously regularly moved around to create new visual and fragrant delights for visitors. Although it was explained to the Europeans that all the roses were being grown in a manner that was 'good Feng Shui', it was to be some years before anyone understood the implications of what they had been told. However, what these foreigners may just have appreciated was that here was a completely new form of gardening which was adaptable and easy to maintain, even in the most cramped conditions. It is possible that in the Fa Tee nurseries, cultivated on Feng Shui lines, the rose garden as we know it today was born.

Of the hybrid China and Tea roses now grown in the West, a number are considered to be good conductors of *Chi* and here is a short list, complete with the date of the flower's introduction:

Yellow: 'Arethusa' (1903), 'Perle d'Or' (1884), 'Adam' (1833), 'Etoile de Lyon' (1881), 'Safrano' (1839).
White: 'Anna-Maria de Montravel' (1880), 'Mme Bravy' (1846), 'Sombreuil' (1850).
Pink: 'Cecile Brunner' (1881), 'Duke of York' (1894), 'Hermosa' (1841), 'L'Ouche' (1901), 'Papillon' (1900), 'Old Blush' (1789), 'Pompon de Paris' (1839), 'Mme Laurette Messimy' (1887).
Red: 'Cramoisi Supérieur' (1832), 'Brennus' (1830), 'Louis XIV' (1859), 'Némésis' (1836), 'Papa Hemeray' (1912), 'Rivers George IV' (1820), 'Fabvier' (1832), 'Miss Lowe's Rose' (1887).

Despite the undeniable worldwide popularity of the rose, in China, as I have said, it is the peony, and in particular the *moutan* or tree peony, that is regarded as the 'King of Flowers'. Its very name—*mou* meaning male and *tan* vermillion—at once suggests the qualities which have been attributed to the blossom: strength, masculinity, aristocracy, wealth and rank. According to Feng Shui these qualities have resulted in the peony being regarded as the flower of *Yang* and a symbol of good fortune. Some Chinese gardeners refer to it as the *fu kuei* (happiness and wealth) or else the *Lo Yang Hua*—the flower of Lo Yang, because it is supposed to have come originally from that city. There is even a lilting poem about the flower, the *Lo Yang Moutan Chi*, which was composed by the great Sung dynasty poet, Ou Yang-hsiu.

Because the spectacular blooms of the peony do not vary, the Chinese have chosen names for them which are based on their colour. Thus the deep red blossoms are referred to as Ink, the white as Jade and the cream as Bright Mountain. The ancient art says that the Ink and another variety with a yellow mark on the petal edge known as 'Golden-border Moutan' are the most highly prized varieties. The peony's finely-shaped, luxuriant leaves are not only delightfully ornamental but good conductors of *Chi*; while for centuries its rough bark has been prescribed for blood disorders.

When the first *moutans* were brought in from the wild for cultivation, they were grown almost exclusively for the emperor and the members of his court. Soon, however, the ordinary people became just as mesmerised by the beautiful flowers, and by the time of the Sung dynasty (tenth to thirteenth centuries) growing them was a kind of national passion throughout China. Evidence suggests that the peony was the very first flower brought into cultivation for pure show.

Feng Shui categorises the peony as a flower of spring. In its native land, the plants are usually positioned all together in beds edged with stone or marble, or in rocky terraces raised on the side of an embankment. This means that when the flowers bloom in early summer they become a focus for both the garden's energy and its human visitors. According to an old tradition, during the days of Imperial China parties were often held in honour of the flowering peonies, and guests would come to drink and chat while admiring the blooms. Not a bad idea to try in the West today, I would suggest.

The lotus follows after the peony as the flower of summer and again is very highly regarded by Feng Shui. In Chinese, the flower, the *Nelumbo nucifera*, is called the *lien* or *ho* flower—*lien* sounding like 'unite' and *ho* resembling the word for 'harmony'. Growing as it does from out of muddy water to spread its green, bowl-shaped leaves and subtle perfume into the air, the lotus is regarded as a symbol of friendship, peace and unity. Confucius saw the radiant purity of the lotus, rising from contamination, as the model for the 'superior man', and agreed with Feng Shui that no garden

FENG SHUI FLORAL CALENDAR

This list of blooms, each symbolising a month of the year, was devised by followers of Feng Shui thousands of years ago and is still observed in many parts of China as well as in Chinese communities all over the world. They are each said to be the ideal floral decoration to promote good Feng Shui in the home and garden in that particular month.

MONTH	FLORAL DECORATION
January	Prunus
February	Peach Blossom
March	Peony
April	Cherry Blossom
May	Magnolia
June	Wisteria
July	Lotus
August	Pear Blossom
September	Mallow
October	Chrysanthemum
November	Gardenia
December	Poppy

lake or pond should be without its blooms to ensure good fortune.

Although growing the lotus is difficult in the West, the plant can be used symbolically as many poor Chinese did, by hanging pictures of it on their walls. It is also regarded as a popular Taoist symbol, being the emblem of one of the Eight Immortals, Ho Hsien-ku. In Chinese literature of the T'ang dynasty are a number of charming descriptions of lotus-gathering ladies harvesting the crop, for the plants were put to many uses other than decoration. The leaves, for example, can be used for flavouring; and the fruit sliced and preserved, to be eaten as a sweetmeat. The rhizomes, too, can be cooked to make a crisp and juicy delicacy, or a starch that is a good remedy for poor digestion. Small wonder that, with its exotic appearance and lingering fragrance, the lotus continues to be so widely grown in China today.

The chrysanthemum, the flower of the autumn, was also originally cultivated for its medicinal and culinary uses rather than as the universally popular ornamental plant it is now. Its reputation seems to have been founded on a legend originating in the town of Nanyang in central China, where it was said that all the people lived to be over one hundred years old. Apparently they all drew their drinking water from a stream where chrysanthemums grew, and it was claimed that the essences of the flowers seeped into the water and gave it its magical powers of longevity. Feng Shui, which says the chrysanthemum is an excellent promoter of energy, also regards the plant as symbolic of long life because it lasts well and blooms in the autumn when most other plants are dying off. In China, tea made from the flower is said to be good for the health, while many generations of country people have made a wine from an infusion of chrysanthemum petals.

The last group of blooms the Chinese hold in greater admiration than the rose are the members of the *Prunus* family such as the cherry and plum trees. Blossoming in the spring, they promise the renewal of vitality and hope, and are very important in regenerating the flow of the earth's energies after the cold winter months. There is a long and moving description in one of the classic Chinese tales of earlier days, the *Yuan Yeh*, about a man standing in a spring snow while he gazes at an array of plum flowers caught in the early morning sunlight. Despite the cold, he feels his heart beginning to flower like the tree, full of vitality and energy. This experience has put him in almost physical touch with the workings of Feng Shui.

However, *Prunus* blossoms and the others are not the only flowers that Feng Shui says are harbingers of good *Chi*. Thanks to information supplied by several experts, I am able to include a list of those plants which are recommended for their beauty, fragrance and harmonious qualities. All came originally from China, but have subsequently been introduced to the West and can be grown in gardens here with just a little care and attention. And by cultivating them singly, or in suitable combinations of *Yin* and *Yang*, it is not too difficult for any horticulturist to create a Feng Shui flower paradise that will be the envy of all who see it.

SHRUBS AND CLIMBERS

Beauty Bush (Meeilih-Tsurng) *Kolkwitzia amabilis*
Element:: *Yin*
Symbolism: *Loveliness*
Like its name, this hardy, deciduous shrub is highly regarded in Feng Shui for its beautiful arching clusters of showy pink flowers with yellow throats which rather resemble small foxgloves. The flowers appear in late spring and bloom until mid-summer to be followed by small, downy seedheads. The matt, dark green leaves are hairy and widely toothed, turning dull red in the autumn, and the brown trunk has an unusual winter feature in that the bark peels away in strips to give an attractive, rather shaggy appearance. Growing easily to a bushy shape up to 3m (10ft) tall and 4m (12ft) wide, the shrub is said to generate the right *Chi* when planted near the house in sun or partial shade in a well-drained soil. It is also good in mixed borders and, according to Feng Shui, makes an ideal partner with the Golden Rain Tree (Huarngjin-Yuh) *Koelreuteria paniculata*. The beauty bush can be propagated from cuttings and the shrubs should be planted in October or March.

Camellia (Charhua) *Camellia* spp.
Element: *Yang*
Symbolism: *Evergreen*
The Chinese say that the camellia has the most attractive leaves of any flowering shrub and its handsome, evergreen and glossy foliage is a good conductor of *Chi* when it is planted against a wall or pruned into a curved hedge. The many species of hardy, evergreen camellia have distinctive

single or double, bowl-shaped flowers in a variety of colours ranging from red to pale pink and white. The *C. reticulata* species, which originated in Western China, is a darker red colour with golden stamens. The early practitioners of Feng Shui were apparently first attracted to the flower because, despite its exotic appearance, it has a remarkable ability to survive harsh winters, coming unfailingly into bloom early in the new year. This quality has subsequently made the camellia popular in the West as an outdoor plant that can be grown in borders or as a pot plant. It requires lime-free soil and grows to a height and spread of 5m (15ft), though in favourable conditions it can attain a height of 15m (50ft). Plant in September and October or in March and April in a part-shady position, sheltered from wind and early morning sun. Dead-head the shrub after flowering and keep well watered in summer. The camellia is also held in high regard in Japan where it is known as 'living jade', and the Chinese make a green tea from a species known as *C. thea* which is sometimes referred to as Ding, after the man who is supposed to have first devised the rather sweet, aromatic drink.

Chinese Jasmine 'Chinese Star' (Luohshya) *Trachelospermum jasminoides*
Element: *Yin*
Symbolism: *Friendship*
The 'Chinese star', with its clusters of delicate, creamy-white flowers and strong, sweet fragrance, has been regarded by the Chinese as a feminine symbol of friendship since the very earliest days. Feng Shui says this climber is ideal for growing around entranceways where it will provide a delightful aroma on entering the garden and smooth the passage of the *Chi*. It also combines well with rock to provide ground cover (in rock gardens), and will twine delightfully over trellises, arbours, pergolas, fences and walls. If planted in full sun in well-drained soil, *T. jasminoides* grows quickly, can reach up to 9m (28ft) tall, and flowers from late June to July; however, it will not survive severe frosts and is a plant

for milder areas of the country. The pretty flowers are offset
by the dark green, oval, evergreen leaves which hang from
twisting vines. The plant can be grown from cuttings, and
shoots layered in September or October can generally be
expected to root within a year. It also benefits from pruning
back the old wood after flowering for revitalisation.

Clematis (Tiee-Shiahn) *Clematis montana*
Element: *Yang*
Symbolism: *Vigour*
This famous climbing species of clematis originated near the
Himalayas where its vigorous growth and large clusters of
star-shaped white flowers were viewed by Feng Shui as ideal
conductors of *Chi*. The deciduous, light-green trifolate leaves
grow on a twining vine with tendrils, and such is its growth
energy that the plant is regarded as one of the easiest flowering climbers to cultivate. The varieties 'Elizabeth' and 'Pink
Perfection' have pink flowers. Initially the clematis tends to
shoot straight up, but then branches at the top and can grow
as much as 1·5–3m (5–10ft) per year. Feng Shui encourages
gardeners to let *C. montana* grow in wavy lines over trelliswork, walls, fences or even posts, and the species can grow
up to 14m (46ft) with a spread of 2–3m (6–10ft). The clematis is best propagated by cuttings planted between October
and May and prefers its roots in a shady spot of well-drained,
fertile soil. Some Feng Shui gardeners recommend planting
a low-growing shrub on the south side of the climber to
provide shade for the roots, while others feel a cluster of
small rocks or pebbles around the stem will have the same
effect. The clematis genus also includes a number of hardy
herbaceous perennials which make good border plants,
including *C. heracleifolia* which originated in China, grows to
about 75cm (30ins) tall, and produces spectacular purple-
blue tubular flowers which bloom in racemes in August and
September. This particular plant has the advantage that
although it is really a sprawling semi-shrub it can be grown
on supports at varying heights in a shrub border to improve
the flow of the *Chi*. Plant in a sunny position between

October and May and, like all herbaceous clematis, it will benefit from an annual spring mulch of compost.

Firethorn (Huoo-Jir) *Pyracantha rogersiana*
Element: *Yin/Yang*
Symbolism: *Nobility*
The dramatic colour change of the firethorn from the profusion of white flowers in the summer months to the equally dense display of red berries which persist throughout the winter from September to March, makes this an excellent example of *Yin* and *Yang* at work. Indeed, some early Chinese gardens were devoted almost solely to firethorn trees arranged around rocks and water pools. The evergreen leaves are thick and glossy and these are complemented by the tiny white hawthorn-like flowers which appear in 5cm (2in) clusters in June. If positioned against a wall, firethorn will require wire for support once the cuttings (or seeds) grow, and it should be planted between October and March in fertile, well-drained soil. The shrub thrives in full sunlight or partial shade and makes an attractive hedge which may require trimming between May and July to ensure it grows into a shape conducive to the flow of the garden's *Chi*. The species *P. angustifolia* and *P. atalantioides* also come from China.

Forsythia (Liarnchiaur) *Forsythia suspensa*
Element: *Yang*
Symbolism: *Energy*
With its bright yellow flowers suspended from a weave of branches, the forsythia was long ago adjudged to encourage the flow of good *Chi* throughout a garden, especially as its flowering announced the arrival of spring. Today this deciduous species, which once bloomed all over China, is regarded worldwide as one of the most popular spring-flowering shrubs that will thrive in most soils and grow well in city gardens. When *F. suspensa* is placed against a wall it can spread 3m (10ft) and more, making a delightful show of its pendulous yellow flowers and broadly ovate, mid-green

leaves. The flowers appear in March in clusters of two and four all along the previous year's shoots and are said by Feng Shui to be symbolic of age supporting and nurturing youth. This species often roots itself when the drooping branches touch the soil, and these rooted layers may be taken from the parent plant in October and, if large enough, put straight into the ground or else cultivated in a nursery bed for a year. Forsythia can be tidied up and shaped in April by removing old and damaged wood with clippers.

Gardenia (Mohlih) *Gardenia augusta*
Element: *Yang*
Symbolism: *Strength*
Although generally only cultivated in greenhouses in the West, the gardenia is a star recommendation by Feng Shui because of its strong fragrance and decorative appearance— it has, of course, been a button-hole favourite for years. The evergreen shrubs came originally from the hot southern climes of China and Japan where it may grow to a height of 12m (40ft) and spread of 3m (10ft), producing white, waxen, heavily scented flowers and dark-green, glossy leaves in whorls of three. The main flowering period is from June to August, but a variety grown indoors called 'Veitchii' blooms in the winter. The plants are best propagated from cuttings in pots of John Innes potting compost in February and March and kept in a humid temperature of 18–21°C (64– 70°F). Gardenias may be planted out in peat in a sunny position from June to mid-September and require frequent watering. When cutting, the flowers should be severed on long stems just as the centre petals are about to open, and after the blooms have finished all growths require shortening by a half to two-thirds.

Hibiscus (Jujinn) *Hibiscus rosa-sinensis*
Element: *Yin*
Symbolism: *Profusion*
The red, star-shaped flowers of the hibiscus with their yellow stamens like inquisitive antennae are acknowledged in Feng

Shui because although they are short-lived (about a day each) they are produced in great numbers from summer to early autumn. This process of constant renewal is believed to be particularly helpful in assisting the flow of the *Chi*, and in many parts of China the hibiscus is a favourite pot plant on balconies and in courtyards where it can reach a height of about 1m (3ft). In the West this plant, like the gardenia, thrives best under glass or as a house plant. The flowers are borne from June to September on the upper leaf axils which are broadly ovate and dark green. A hardier species like *H. syriacus*, which comes in red, purple, blue and white, can be grown from seeds or cuttings planted from October to March in a sunny position in a humus-rich soil, and as one of the last shrubs to leaf in the spring offers the compensation of continuing to flower when many other blooms in the garden have long since faded. Growing to over 3m (10ft), it can make an attractive hedge or even a small lawn feature.

Honeysuckle (Reendung) *Lonicera nitida*
Element: *Yin*
Symbolism: *Faithfulness*
This species of honeysuckle is a dense, evergreen shrub which will make a fine hedge and is suitable for mixed and shrub borders. Feng Shui recognises the power of *L. nitida* to grow in the shade, and although its creamy-white flowers which open in April and May are small, they are followed by striking semi-translucent violet or amethyst globular berries which some Chinese have said bear a marked resemblance to the *Yin* and *Yang* symbol. The plant with its ovate and glossy dark green leaves, also has a distinctive fragrance when in flower, which has long made it a favourite with Chinese ladies. The shrub should be put in ordinary well-drained soil between September and March and mulched with compost once a year in the spring. If *L. nitida* is intended to be used to form a hedge, the young plants are best set at intervals of 23–30cm (9–12ins). Another species, *L. tragophylla* (often called 'Chinese Woodbine') is noted for its ovate leaves, dark green on top and glaucous-white beneath. These provide

a fine background for the terminal whorls of the plant's spectacular golden-yellow flowers which Feng Shui says are excellent conductors of good *Chi*.

Hydrangea (Tuu-Charngshan) *Hydrangea macrophylla*
Element: *Yang*
Symbolism: *Achievement*
With heart-shaped light green leaves and lacy clusters of blue blooms, the Chinese hydrangea has long been a favourite in the garden as well as looking good in arrangements of fresh flowers. The rounded, deciduous shrubs which bloom through the summer to early autumn are ideal for town gardens and reach a height and spread of 2m (6ft). The hydrangea prefers to be in full sun in well-drained, loamy soil, and the colour of the flower will depend on the soil's pH factor. A neutral or alkaline soil will produce pink flowers, while the blue flowers require an acid soil. *H. macrophylla* can be grown from cuttings taken during June or July, which should be planted out in October and November or March and April. Some Feng Shui gardeners claim the finest blue blooms are those grown beneath the canopy of a tree, where they are also useful at channelling the *Chi*. A popular garden form of this species is 'Blue Bonnet' with its excellent rounded shape and luxurious blue florets, which also meets the requirements of Feng Shui.

Lilac (Bairdingshiang) *Syringa pubescens* sbsp. *microphylla*
Element: *Yang*
Symbolism: *Virility*
This handsome shrub can be grown as an informal hedge or screen or in shrub borders or a rock garden for which it is ideally suited, according to Feng Shui. The aromatic, lilac-coloured flowers appear in panicles during the month of June and again in September. The ovate mid-green leaves of this species are also distinguishable by their downy covering. Long ago the ancient art discovered that the lilac thrived as well in towns as it does in the countryside, and it is recommended for the West where it is said to grow hardily in the

city, even in areas of high pollution. Cuttings of *microphylla* should be planted between October and November in sun or partial shade in any fertile garden soil and the plant will take a year or two to establish itself. For hedges and screens set young plants at about 1·5–3m (5–10ft) apart; and the shrubs can be rejuvenated by cutting out weak branches during the winter. Another species, *S. reflexa*, also originated in China and grows fragrant, deep pink flowers which appear in June.

Peony (Muh-Shauryauh) *Paeonia suffruticosa*
Element: *Yang*
Symbolism: *Wealth*
The tree peony has been *the* great favourite of the Chinese for centuries, and in Feng Shui it is recognised for its sumptuous beauty and its ability to keep bad *Sha* at bay. In parts of Western China where it originated, the tree peony is also held to be a divine plant that can drive off evil spirits, while its seeds were once used to spice recipes and its roots, powdered and infused, were a cure for liver complaints. The single, double and semi-double flowers of *P. suffruticosa*, which open in May, grow up to 30cm (12ins) across and have clusters of yellow stamens which contrast markedly with the white, yellow, pink, red or purple petals. The graceful grey-green leaves contribute to the plant's height and spread of 2·2m (7ft) which make it excellent in mixed or shrub borders. The peony prefers to be in shade in a well-drained soil, and although it takes a while to become established, once settled it can be left undisturbed for 50 years or more. Plant during mild weather between September and March (seeds in the autumn only) and mulch annually in April. Some modern Feng Shui gardeners in the West particularly recommend a subspecies, *rockii*, called 'Joseph Rock', with pure white flowers and a prominent maroon-crimson blotch at the base of each petal, which they believe is symbolic of a bond between the plant and the earth and representative of good *Chi*.

Redbud (Chyh-Leei) *Cercis chinensis*
Element: *Yang*
Symbolism: *Romance*
The redbud, with its rose-pink, pea-shaped flowers and heart-shaped, shiny, dark green leaves is seen by Feng Shui as an ideal companion for a sturdy garden tree and can also serve as an excellent solo feature. The flower clusters, which measure 15mm (½in) across, blossom like new love on the naked, branching stems in late spring, while the deciduous leaves turn yellow in the autumn, giving the redbud a charming appeal throughout much of the year. *C. chinensis* has an open, bushy appearance and grows to 6m (20ft). As suggested by its name, the redbud likes to be positioned in full sunlight in a well-drained, loamy soil. It can be grown from cuttings which should be put into the ground in late September and October or April and May. The tree requires no pruning.

Rhododendron (Nauhyarnghua) *Rhododendron* spp.
Element: *Yin*
Symbolism: *Delicacy*
This is a genus of hundreds of species of evergreen and deciduous shrubs, including azaleas which were formerly treated as a separate genus. Although the name rhododendron comes from the Greek *rhodon* (rose) and *dendron* (tree), the majority of this genus, which is now so popular with gardeners all over the world, originated in China. Feng Shui again attaches importance to the use of the rhododendron in rock gardens, as well as in mixed or shrub borders; its rounded flower clusters in white, yellow, pink, red and purple, and large, smooth, oval green leaves splayed out in a fan shape, combine to form a wide, billowing shape ideally suited as a conductor of *Chi*. In the wild some species may reach a height of 25m (80ft). The azalea, which is a lower, more compact shrub, with smaller leaves and flowers, has a similar colour range with the addition of orange, apricot and crimson, and is also said to be an aid to a garden's Feng Shui with its funnel-shaped flowers and leaves set in light-green whorls. Both like

semi-shaded spots in moist but well-drained, leafy, humus-rich acid soil and bloom from spring to early summer. The rhododendron can be grown from seed (sown in February or March), layering (any time of the year), or cuttings (from mid-July to late August), and requires no pruning beyond deadheading with finger and thumb. Because of its compact root system, Feng Shui advises transplanting a rhododendron to a new position rather than pruning it if it is not helping the flow of *Chi* in the garden. The azalea is ideal for city locations as it has a good toleration of air pollution.

Rose (Muhshiang) 'Old Blush China' (*Rosa chinensis* var.)
Element: *Yin*
Symbolism: *Beauty*
If dedicated Feng Shui gardeners with only the minimum of ground space at their disposal were asked to pick one rose to enhance the *Chi* in their garden, the majority would probably agree upon the airy, graceful 'Old Blush' with its loose sprays of small, sweetly-scented blooms which continue flowering from June to Christmas. The plant is famous in Britain as the subject of Thomas Moore's famous poem 'The Last Rose of Summer', and for the tribute from Dean Hole who called it the 'brave old Monthly' that was 'the last to yield in winter and first to bloom in summer'. Apart from its historical associations as one of the earliest China roses—first reported in Hupeh, according to legend—the plant can cope with differing temperatures and is ideal for providing the finishing touch to any small garden bed. 'Old Blush' is said to combine happily with azaleas, clematis and wisteria—all recognised for their good Feng Shui qualities—and with an average height and width of 1·2m (4ft) is suitable for just about every property. As pleasing to the eye as it is to the earth energies, 'Old Blush' is covered in rosy-pink flowers which deepen with age and there are generally several shades of pink, rose and pale carmine on the bush, creating a chintz-like effect against the green of the older leaves and the reddish brown tones of the young shoots. The fragrance of its fresh scent is an added garden delight in mid-winter.

'Old Blush' grows best in a sunny position (preferably facing south) and likes a well-drained soil. The plant is easy to grow, but it does benefit from having the spent blooms cut off and the occasional removal of old wood right from the base.

Wisteria (Terng) *Wisteria sinensis*
Element: *Yin*
Symbolism: *Beauty*
Feng Shui recommends combining wisteria with rhododendrons and roses, and considers it one of the most versatile of plants because it can be treated as a shrub, a tree or even a vine! The Chinese wisteria is not generally said to be as spectacular as the Japanese variety, *W. floribunda*, with its red, purple, pink or white trumpet-shaped flowers, but nonetheless its long 30cm (12ins) racemes of fragrant mauve flowers can still dramatically improve the appearance of a fence or wall when allowed to sprawl over the wood or brickwork. The flowers in May and June before the foliage is fully developed. The young plants should be set out between October and March during a time of mild weather and prefer a sunny spot with well-drained, loamy soil. Once established, wisteria should be cut back in late summer and again in February, to within two or three buds of the base of the previous year's growth, to restore vitality and stimulate growth. The *W. sinensis* species has dark to mid-green leaves which consist of up to 13 leaflets. A variety, 'Alba', has the prettiest white flowers which also hang in luscious racemes. In the opinion of many Feng Shui experts, no garden is complete—or properly equipped to attract good *Chi*—if it does not contain at least one wisteria correctly sited.

HERBACEOUS PLANTS

Aster (Shing-Tsaai) *Callistephus chinensis* cultivars
Element: *Yang*
Symbolism: *Elegance*
These brightly-coloured, daisy-like flowers, ranging in colour from golden yellow to deep purple, are said to be ideal

conductors of good *Chi* when in their full glory. Elegant in appearance with neat green leaves, the plants take their common name from the Greek *aster* for star, but in China they are said to symbolise the majesty of the sun and heavens. *C. chinensis* is just one of hundreds of species of aster— annuals, biennials, perennials and subshrubs—which are suitable for cultivating in borders or rock gardens. Cultivars of *C. chinensis* range from 20cm (8ins) to 75cm (30ins) in height and are best situated in a large group of a single colour in a sunny position that has well-drained soil. The flowers open in early summer and bloom for about four weeks. *C. chinensis* makes excellent cut flowers, cuttings from a single group providing more than enough for a fine indoor display.

Chinese lantern (Jungguor Deng'Lung) *Physalis franchetii*
Element: *Yang*
Symbolism: *Illumination*
The Chinese lantern as we known it in the West has thrived in China for untold years, where its white flowers, which turn into bright golden, inflated, lantern-like calyces, are believed to represent the dawning of understanding and illumination in each of the generations of mankind. Sometimes called a 'bladder cherry', the lantern with its wavy mid-green leaves can grow from 60–70cm (24–30ins) in well-drained, sandy soil and is noted for its ability to spread invasively. *P. franchetii* should be planted in March or April, and the small flowers will bloom in July and August to be followed by the papery 'lanterns' which are actually seed cases enclosing an edible orange-red berry—though I do not recommend eating it! To use the lanterns for decoration, they must be picked before the colour turns and the stems should be hung in a light, airy room. Feng Shui says the Chinese lantern is best grown on its own, but where it is sited in a mixed bed or border it may well be necessary to cut off the invasive underground runners with a spade and dig them out. With its golden colour which is so highly rated by the ancient art, *P. franchetii* is ideal both for growing outdoors and showing indoors.

Chrysanthemum (Chuh) *Chrysanthemum morifolium*
Element: *Yang*
Symbolism: *Resolution*

C. morifolium, which originated in Northern China, is the parent of a great many of the border perennials and half-hardy greenhouse plants, ranging from daisylike flowers to huge globular heads, which are sold today by florists all over the world. Known originally as the 'Queen of the Autumn', the chrysanthemum was early recruited as a temple ornament as well as a decoration to be painted on porcelain, hammered onto metal and embroidered in brocades. A legendary Feng Shui *xiansheng*, Tao Ming-Yang, is credited with having improved the colour and form of many varieties of this plant, and after his death his fellow citizens commemorated his work by naming their town 'Chuh-sien', the City of Chrysanthemums. Interestingly, when the flower was first introduced to England in the eighteenth century there was considerable controversy over where it had originated in the Orient; this was eventually resolved by calling it *Chrysanthemum sinense*, 'the Golden Flower from China.'

C. morifolium grows in attractive mounds 30–60cm (12–24ins) high and in colours ranging from white, yellow and bronze to orange, red, lavender and purple. It flourishes from cuttings or division and likes to be in full sun in a well-drained and fertile soil. The blooms of the chrysanthemum last from midsummer to the autumn frosts, and apart from looking good in mixed beds and borders, their cascades of flowers and dark green leaves make them ideal for potting on balconies and patios where they can help influence a garden's Feng Shui. They make excellent cut flowers, too—the golden varieties are good conductors of *Chi* in any house or apartment. To maintain the rounded look of the chrysanthemum plant it should be carefully shaped in spring and summer. As a matter of note, in China some chrysanthemums are still referred to by their original, charming names: for example, yellow varieties are called 'Heaven full of Stars'; the varieties with fine petals, 'Pine Needles' or 'Dragon's Beard'; those that are white streaked with red, 'Snow on the Ground', the idea being that of a young girl admiring the snow; and, most delightful of all, the large, ragged mauve chrysanthemums are known as 'Drunk-with-Wine-made-from-Peaches-of-the-Immortals'!

Garden balsam (Jyy'Jia) *Impatiens balsamina*
Element: *Yin*
Symbolism: *Tenderness*
The garden balsam is a species generally better suited to the warm southern climes of China than the colder regions of the West, because it is a half-hardy plant that can be killed by frost. Nonetheless, Feng Shui regards it as a plant that symbolises tenderness, with its warm colours of white, pink and purple—although it has to be said it does not stand up well to wet and cold weather. The compact balsam, which grows to about 75cm (30ins), will deflect the harmful *Sha* when planted in a sunny, sheltered spot in a humus-rich soil. Its delightful cup-shaped flowers blossom from June to September on pale green leaves. *I. balsamina* is best propagated from seeds which can be sown directly into the garden in March or April or, if there is a possibility of bad weather, under cover and grown on for about six weeks before transplanting into a suitable bed. Many readers will already be familiar with the hybrids of *I. walleriana*, and the New Guinea hybrids which are commonly sold as 'busy lizzies'.

Hollyhock (Rurngkueir) *Alcea rosea*
Element: *Yin*
Symbolism: *Ambition, uprightness*
The popular hollyhock was formerly known as *A. chinensis* and in its native China has for centuries been highly regarded medicinally for its ability to soothe all parts of the body, as well as an indispensable ornament of walled gardens. Its combination of beauty and tall, robust pillars of widely funnel-shaped flowers, with their three-lobed light green leaves, makes it a good conductor of *Chi* when the plant is grown at the rear of annual or herbaceous borders. Interestingly, the hollyhock was first introduced into

England as a pot herb, but became a cottage garden favourite due to its wide variety of colours, ranging from deep crimson, scarlet and violet to pink, yellow and white. The plant can be cultivated from seed or cuttings and likes to grow in full sun in a heavy, rich soil. It grows from 1·5–2·5m (5–8ft) and blooms spectacularly through mid to late summer. The hollyhock requires plenty of watering during dry weather, and it can be grown as a biennial by sowing in midsummer to flower the following year. Feng Shui lore says that the hollyhock combines well with other species of mallow (Malvaceae) to bring vitality to a garden.

Orchid (Larnhua) *Bletilla striata*
Element: *Yang*
Symbolism: *Endurance*
Although numerous species of orchid have been cultivated in China since the earliest times, *B. striata* is perhaps the only one which can be successfully grown in the West as an aid to Feng Shui. Groups of this orchid with clusters of tall pink, lavender, purple and occasionally white flowers amidst their prominent dark green leaves, will grow into attractive clumps 30–60cm (12–24ins) tall, and bloom in early summer. The plant has underground pseudobulbs that look rather like flattened globular tubers and these should be cultivated in a well-drained soil enriched with peat or leaf-mould. September and October are the best months to propagate the orchid by clump division, and in cold districts it should be protected during the winter months with a covering of sand or weathered ashes. *B. striata* makes a good pot plant and when cut will last far longer than many other blooms. The flowers are also, incidentally, almost perfect miniatures of the familiar florist's orchid known as *Cattleya* (Orchidaceae).

Pinks (Shyrjur) *Dianthus chinensis*
Element: *Yang*
Symbolism: *Good luck*
D. chinensis is one of the most beautiful low-growing plants among the genus of several hundred species which include

the well known pinks, carnations and sweet william. This particular pink grows in masses of scented single or double frilled flowers in colours from white to red, lavender, purple and bicolour, against a foliage of slim, silvery-green leaves which will remain attractive in gardens in mildish climates throughout the winter when the plant's hardiness enables it to become a perennial. *D. chinensis* is sometimes called 'Rainbow Pink' and when propagated from seeds or cuttings or by dividing existing plants, and placed in a sunny, well-drained soil, will grow up to 70cm (28ins) tall depending on the variety. The gentle mounds of pinks which flower from July to mid-to-late autumn are said by Feng Shui to be good conductors of *Chi*, and it especially recommends them for rock gardens. The flowers are also ideal for use in floral arrangements. *D. chinensis* is esteemed by Feng Shui experts because of the intricate, weaving markings which are found on the petals of many individual flowers.

Poppy (Yingsuh) *Papaver orientale*
Element: *Yin*
Symbolism: *Pleasure*
This perennial, one of the hundred-odd species of Papaveraceae, is said by Feng Shui to be good for mixed and herbaceous borders, and particularly larger rock gardens where the characteristic bowl shape of the flowers combines with the shape of the rocks to aid the flow of *Chi*. A hardy, cheering plant, it has deeply cut, mid to deep green leaves and brilliantly coloured, giant, paper-like red flowers with a black spot at the base of each petal. These burst into bloom in late spring or early summer. The many cultivars range in colour from white to orange, pink, red and bicolour. *P. orientale* grows to a height of 45–90cm (18–36ins), likes a sunny position and will flourish in any well-drained soil. It should be planted in October or March and will need staking as it grows, as well as dead-heading after flowering. It is important to site a poppy carefully (it can be grown by seeds, root cuttings or division in late summer) because root disturbance may cause it to die. Its leaves turn brown in mid-

summer but reappear in the autumn and then stay green throughout the winter. The poppy may well produce a few more flowers in the autumn if the first flower stems are cut back, and thereby provide a little more colour and pleasure at the onset of winter. The poppy makes a good cut flower and Feng Shui says the seed pods will enhance the *Chi* potential of any dried floral arrangement.

Primula (Yingtsaav) *Primula sinensis*
Element: *Yang*
Symbolism: *Virtue*
The outstanding colour range of *P. sinensis*, and the fact that it can be grown both indoors (as a pot plant) and outdoors (in moist, acid soil), have made its spread from northern China both inevitable and welcome. Thick stems about 30cm (12ins) tall carry two or three whorls of flowers from a rosette of mid-green leaves close to the soil, blooming from late spring to midsummer in the garden, December to March indoors. Another species which will grow more easily outdoors is *P. flaccida* which originated in Yunnan. It is much the same size, has grey-green leaves but scented flowerheads of lavender-violet bells which appear in June. There is also a species of border primula belonging to the Candelabra group—notably *P. denticuluta*, the 'Drumstick Primula'—possessing a colour range from pale lilac to deep purple and rose to deep carmine, which are said by Feng Shui to be good for rock gardens, and especially for waterside planting. They thrive along pond margins and can be planted between October and March. If used in an ordinary border, however, it is important to ensure the 'Drumstick Primula' is kept moist by regular watering.

Tiger lily (Jyuaandan) *Lilium lancifolium* (syn. *L. tigrinum*)
Element: *Yang*
Symbolism: *Pride*
Because of the traditional alliance of the tiger and the dragon, which is the basis of Feng Shui, *L. lancifolium* or 'Tiger Lily' as it is best known, is highly regarded by the

ancient art. In China, where it first grew, the bulbs of the plant were steamed or boiled as food, and it was also used medicinally for stomach pains and headaches. The recurved Turk's cap flowers, with bright orange petals speckled with purple-black spots and prominent anthers of dark red pollen, are the focal point of the plant against its pointed mid-green leaves. The 'Tiger Lily' should be planted in full sun in lime-free soil and it will grow to 0·6–1·5m (2–5ft), blooming in August and September. The plant is easy to propagate by using the black bulblets that form in the leaf axils, or alternatively by division. The nodding heads of this species are among the best conductors of *Chi*, according to Feng Shui, and no dedicated follower of the art would have a garden without a clump of the flowers—perhaps as a background plant in a mixed bed or a border. The Tiger Lily also makes a fine cut flower and can be an additional element to enhance the harmony of your home.

6 *THE ENERGY OF TREES*

'If a home has not a garden and an old tree, I see not whence
the everyday joys of life are to come,' wrote an ancient
Chinese horticulturist named Ch'en Hao-tsu. His love of
trees and flowers was beautifully expressed in his essays and
poems and ultimately earned him the epithet of the 'Flower
Hermit'. He was a lifelong believer in Feng Shui, too, and
shared its philosophy that trees possess powers of energy
which can be utilised by those who appreciate them to ensure
harmony and well-being in their lives and homes.

The Chinese have held trees in great esteem since the
very earliest times, believing that, as their different colours
of green unfold, they create private, enclosed spaces in the
area around them—yet in such a way that is the very opposite
of claustrophobic. And as their leaves and branches sway in
the breeze, conducting the *Chi* as they do so, the trees generate constantly changing pictures of light and shade that will
delight and calm in equal measure. In other words, trees
are said to create for mankind a mysterious and magical
expansion of space.

A number of Chinese philosophers have described the
role of trees in a garden as rather like that of clothes on
men and women. They can enhance some areas, obscure

others and in certain places totally alter the appearance of the forms beneath. And when trees and flowers are combined in a balanced and harmonious style they provide the garden with a 'dress' equal to any that might be worn by a human being.

Long ago, trees were regarded as the natural guardians of the dead and, as the history of ancient China records, were considered inviolate much as they were in the temple arboretums of Egypt. It was the custom to surround family graves with trees, and eventually these grew into groves. Indeed, it is probably fair to say that many a coppice in the countryside of China today had its beginnings in this reverence for ancestors and the dead.

China can lay claim to what is believed to be the oldest tree in the world, dating back to the Jurassic period. Readers are probably familiar with the languid willow tree which has always been a favourite in its native China and is generally assumed to be the tree represented on the world-famous 'Willow Pattern' china. However, an increasing number of students of Oriental history believe the gnarled old tree on the pattern may actually be the *Ginkgo biloba* or maidenhair tree. It is an ancient tree that has been described as 'a living fossil' because it has no closer relatives than those found in fossilised form.

This dating suggests that the tree had its heyday millions of years ago, in that period of the world's history when giant reptiles like the dinosaur roamed the earth. Curiously, the *Ginkgo* has never been seen growing wild in any part of the world, although it is cultivated all over China and is especially associated with palaces, temples and other ancient sites. It is often referred to as the world's oldest nut tree and for centuries has been grown for its seeds—known as 'white' or 'silver' nuts. In the West, the maidenhair tree has nowadays become something of a feature in city parks, large town gardens and cathedral closes.

Feng Shui believes that trees in general are some of the best examples of the transforming powers of nature, and that we should all be aware of their magic. While many people in the West are understandably concerned with establishing bonds with other human beings, the ancient art believes we should also acknowledge the importance of trees in our lives. For despite the growing concern for ecology, people on the whole do not seem fully to appreciate how reliant humanity is upon trees, and how the survival of one species depends on the survival of others. This is what Feng Shui has maintained for centuries: that trees themselves provide a living energy that can enhance the *Chi* of any garden.

In the West we have a subconscious feeling for the power of trees, evident in the old superstition that to 'touch wood' will bring us good luck. In China there is an equally common saying, *Da shu zhe yin*, meaning that a big tree gives shade. Feng Shui has taken that concept farther to show that trees, because of their inherent energy, can shield people as well as buildings from bad environmental influences. If they are growing in the wrong place, however, they can obstruct the *Chi* to a detrimental extent. Indeed, our *Yin* and *Yang* relationship with the trees around us will determine the effect they have upon our lives. To take just two simple examples: a withering or dead tree in line with the front door of a house is bad Feng Shui because it harbours *Sha*, while a tree, or group of trees, placed towards the rear of the garden on the dragon (left) side near the phoenix (rear) aspect will encourage good *Chi* to remain within the garden.

Feng Shui says that without trees, humanity would not have the air to breathe (because they process carbon dioxide into oxygen), rain for crops (which is generated by tracts of forestland) or, through the use of their wood, the means to build a shelter and keep warm. To these we must add that many different species of tree have provided us with beauty, food and medicine. The early *xiansheng* drew parallels between trees and mankind, saying that both 'stand' upright on the earth and have their 'heads' in the air. The fact that many trees are taller than us, and most live a lot longer, only serves to enhance their perceived powers.

The old sages also commented upon the ability of trees to improve the well-being of people, because a number pos-

According to Feng Shui, trees can be great generators of energy in a garden.

sessed quite remarkable healing properties. Willow trees, for example, are said to reduce blood pressure and strengthen the bladder, while the maple is good for the relief of pain. The dove tree (*Davidia*) is, of course, one of the oldest known safeguards against evil spirits, and on an emotional level plum trees are believed to exert a soothing influence on the nerves.

Today scientists have actually established what Feng Shui understood long ago—that trees give out negative ions, elec-tromagnetic emissions that can make us feel better when we are near them. Michael Josh, a former research scientist who now runs an environmental charity, the Bridge Educational Trust, in Cumbria, has explained it in these words: 'Everything that is alive is surrounded by electromagnetic fields, so it is simply a case of conduction. If we have too much stored energy which could make us unwell, it will be taken by the tree into the air or absorbed through the roots in the ground. Likewise, if we feel run down, a tree can emit extra energy to us. I believe there are lots of benefits to be gained by simply aligning your back with a tree.'

Feng Shui, for its part, claims that *where* a tree grows in the wild can also determine its effect on people and places. Those that grow near running water symbolise movement and have the power to bolster flagging energy; while those beside still water can induce a feeling of calmness. Any trees growing in large fields are also said to by symbolic of peacefulness.

An early Western account of the philosophy of Feng Shui as it is practised in the planting of trees in China is to be found in Sir William Chambers' book *A Dissertation on Oriental Gardening* (1772), in which he writes that 'their practice is guided by many rules, *founded on reason and long observation* [my italics] from which they seldom or never deviate.' He goes on:

> *The perfection of trees for ornamental gardening*: consists in their size, in the beauty and variety of their forms, the colour and character of their bark, the quantity, shape, and rich verdure of their foliage, with its early appearance in the spring, and long duration in the autumn; likewise in the quickness of their growth, and their hardiness to endure the extremities of heat, cold, drought or moisture; in their making no litter, during the spring or summer, by the fall of blossom; and the strength of their branches to resist, unhurt, the violence of tempests.
>
> *The perfection of shrubs*: consists not only in most of the above mentioned particulars, but also in the beauty,

durability, or long succession of their blossom, and in their appearance before the bloom and after it is gone. We are sensible, they say, that no plant is possessed of all good qualities, but choose such as have the fewest faults, and avoid all those that vegetate with difficulty in our climate.

The excessive variety of which some European gardeners are so fond in their gardens, the Chinese blame; observing that a great diversity of colours, foliage and direction of branches must create confusion, and destroy all the masses upon which effect and grandeur depend. They observe, too, that it is unnatural; for, as in nature most plants sow their own seeds, whole forests are generally composed of the same sort of trees. They admit, however, of a moderate variety; but are by no means indiscriminate in the choice of their trees, attending with great care to the colour, form and foliage of each, and only mixing together such as *harmonise and assemble agreeably* [my italics].

The Chinese observe that some trees are only proper for thickets; others only fit to be employed singly; and others equally adapted to both these situations. The mountain cedar, the spruce and silver firs, and all others whose branches have a horizontal direction, they hold improper for thickets because they indent into each other and likewise press disagreeably upon the plants which back them. They never mix these horizontal-branched trees with the cypress, the oriental *arbor vitae*, the bamboo, or other upright ones; nor with the larch, the weeping willow, the birch, the laburnum, or any of a pendant nature, observing that the intersection of their branches forms a very unpicturesque kind of network. Neither do they employ together the catalpa and the acacia, the yew and the willow, the plane and the sumach, nor any of such heterogeneous sorts; but on the contrary they assemble in their large woods the oak, the elm, the beech, the tupelo, the sycamore, maple and plane, the chestnut, the walnut, the abele,

the lime and all those whose luxuriant foliage hides the
direction of their branches; and growing in globular
masses, assemble well together; forming, by their harmonious combination of their tints, one grand group
of rich verdure.

What is evident from this account is just how very firmly
entrenched the idea of harmony was in the way the Chinese
planted their trees. Feng Shui also emphasises that trees in
gardens should have soft outlines which will enable a viewer's
eyes to be led harmoniously across the landscape. Those
trees which are more gracious—such as the magnolias,
maples and the willow—and therefore *Yin*, should take pride
of place in any Western garden to ensure good *Chi*; trees
with harsh, angular outlines, like conifers, firs and cypress,
are not recommended by the experts unless a person hap-
pens to live in a mountainous part of the country.

As a general rule, trees should never be too close to a
house not only because they may cast too much shade, but
also because the roots may undermine the building, causing
subsidence, although this alone is unlikely to cause damage
unless the tree is growing in a shrinkable, heavy clay soil
affected by prolonged dry weather.

Feng Shui advises against cutting down mature trees unless
absolutely necessary. The trees have stood there for years
and will have developed their own relationship with the *Chi*
and the way it circulates around them. The older and more
gnarled a tree, the less a gardener should be tempted to
remove it because, like the revered *Ginkgo*, it has a long
tradition of fostering the earth energies. If any tree has
become an eyesore, then it is better to train a climber over
it than take up an axe, says Feng Shui in a protective manner
that would surely have been appreciated by George Wash-
ington.

The taller trees for a garden should be chosen with great
care, especially if the plot is a small one, because if they are
too tall or too spreading, they will severely restrict what can
be grown beneath them. Some trees can grow very fast and

their branches may intrude into the space of neighbouring gardens or their roots crack walls, so it is a good idea to consult an expert about the growth patterns of any tree before planting it. Since there is a premium on space in the average garden, a tree has to work hard for its keep and should ideally provide a rewarding picture in several seasons—attractive foliage in spring, flowers and/or fruit in summer, good autumn colour and graceful branches in winter. Feng Shui considers flowering crab apples particularly valuable in this respect.

Trees with attractive bark, like the lacebark pine, are also good for the smaller garden. If the plant is an evergreen, it will provide a permanent structural feature, although too many evergreens can create a very dense, solid feel which will encourage *Sha*. The most interesting Feng Shui gardens are undoubtedly those that contain a mixture of evergreens and deciduous trees and shrubs.

Always remember that carefully sited trees will provide shelter and protection for the garden as well as enhancing its *Chi* quality. If they are planted in varied and staggered positions they will serve as primary forces to combat the straight lines of walls or fences which are bad Feng Shui.

A couple of final points before we reach the list of trees recommended for their Feng Shui qualities. The ancient art is opposed to bonsai trees because it says deliberately stunted growth is against nature. It also maintains that ornamental fruit trees are actually better conductors of *Chi* than the ordinary edible varieties—which, I suppose, is good news for very small gardens. Having said this, I do still believe that there should be a place for an apple tree, and perhaps even my own favourite, the apricot.

A garden in Peking in which trees play a central role in generating good *Chi*.

GARDEN TREES

Dove tree (Lirngtz-Muh) *Davidia involucrata*
Element: *Yin*
Symbolism: *Peacefulness*
The broad, pyramid shaped *D. involucrata* is known in some parts of China as the 'ghost tree' because of its appearance, but it has the reputation of being a protector against evil. Feng Shui says that the bright green heart-shaped leaves with their silky undersides, and the white floral bracts which look like a flock of doves resting in the branches (or a gathering of phantoms, depending on your inclination), are a good source of defence against bad *Sha*. The tree, which originated in central and western China, is also noted for its finely flaking reddish-brown bark and the profusion of flowers that

decorate it spectacularly from May onwards once it is ten years and older. It can grow up to 15m (50ft) tall with a spread of 10m (30ft). Propagation can be done from seed and the tree prefers a shaded area with well-drained soil. Feng Shui says it makes an excellent lawn feature and can be used in a *Yin/Yang* partnership with darker, more towering trees such as the pine. Once difficult to obtain in the West, *D. involucrata* (which has earned a third name in Britain as the 'handkerchief tree') is now available at garden centres and with its exotic blooms will undoubtedly enhance even the smallest garden.

Golden rain tree (Huarngjin-Yuh) *Koelreuteria paniculata*
Element: *Yang*
Symbolism: *Resilience*
The golden rain tree with its beautiful yellow, star-shaped flowers which bloom early in the summer, retains its energy deep into the autumn while producing papery seed pods. Feng Shui values this resilience in the tree, especially because it can thrive in difficult soils, poor weather conditions and even a polluted atmosphere. Indeed, it makes a good street tree and can be grown successfully on a barren or poor quality lawn. *K. paniculata* is sparsely branched when young, has light-brown bark, and leaves which are mid-green until they take on a yellow tint in the autumn. The fruit of the golden rain tree is located in a papery bladder holding three black seeds, and this becomes flushed with a conspicuous red colour in the autumn. The tree grows remarkably quickly into a billowing shape about 10m (30ft) in height and spread. It can be cultivated from ripe seeds sown in October or by cuttings taken in March. The sun glinting through the branches of a mature golden rain tree has delighted many a Feng Shui gardener over the centuries, bringing pleasure to his soul and harnessing good *Chi* for his land.

Magnolia (Muhbii) *Magnolia denudata*
Element: *Yin*
Symbolism: *Fragrance*
Of the almost one hundred species of magnolia, *M. denudata*
is considered to be among the most fragrant and spectacular
with its white, chalice-shaped flowers and mid-green, ovate
leaves that are white and downy on the underside. The
smooth, silver-grey bark and the curves of the branches only
enhance the Feng Shui of this very popular tree. With an
eventual height and spread of 10m (30ft), the tree, which
bears its showy flowers in profusion from March to May,
originated in south-west China where it was often grown near
the entrance to a building in order to conduct in good *Chi.*
The magnolia can be planted in March (with supporting
stakes for a few years) in well-drained, loamy soil in an appropriate site—but one that must be sheltered from north and
east winds. Seeds should be propagated from October in a
peaty compost and allowed to grow for 12–18 months, when
the seedlings should be hardy enough to put outdoors. This
species does not grow quickly, but in its mature years is said
by the Chinese to be almost unequalled in the sense of pride
it can give to a garden and, by inference, those who live
there.

Maidenhair tree or Ginkgo (Gung-Shuh) *Ginkgo biloba*
Element: *Yin/Yang*
Symbolism: *Friendship*
The ancient ginkgo, mentioned earlier in this chapter, is a
deciduous tree with fan-shaped green leaves that are not
unlike those found on some pear trees. According to Feng
Shui, the tree is believed to attract friendship to the owner
of the land on which it stands. Each ginkgo is either male
or female and can grow to a height of 30m (100ft) with a
spread of 8m (25ft), making it a tree for larger gardens
only. First recorded in cultivation in Chekiang province, the
male trees produce thick, yellow catkins, while the female
flowers grow in pairs and are rather like tiny, long-stalked
acorns. The subsequent fruits are plum-shaped with a

smooth, pale green skin which ripens in autumn to yellow
and then brown. They are not edible. The maidenhair can
only be raised from seeds which must be sown as soon
as ripe. This should be carried out not later than October
in a cold frame or greenhouse and then planted out the
following October to March in a warm, sunny position—
although the tree is actually hardy enough to withstand
moderate exposure. Chinese gardeners recommend letting
the young tree grow for three or four years before planting
it in its final position in early April. A warm climate encourages the maidenhair tree which, with its irregular
branches and a bark that is fissured and fluted, is a good
conductor of *Chi*. Feng Shui warns never to prune the ginkgo
as shortened shoots will die back, just as a friendship can
wither.

Paper-bark maple (Hurng) *Acer griseum*
Element: *Yin*
Symbolism: *Success*
Discovered centuries ago in central China, the paper-bark
maple is now found in Western gardens of all sizes, where
its peeling dark-red or rich chestnut bark is complemented
by the green leaves which turn red and scarlet in autumn,
giving the tree a most striking and distinguished appearance.
Feng Shui considers this one of the most decorative of foliage
trees, creating an atmosphere of style and success in any
garden, as well as being a firm defender against bad *Sha*.
The small yellow-green flowers open in May and hang in
bunches, and the seeds (or keys) have prominent wings—
symbolic of the 'flight' of success, according to Feng Shui—
although they are seldom fertile. *A. griseum* can be grown
from seed sown in October, or may be planted from October
to March in well-drained, moist soil. To get the full effect
of the leaf colours it should be positioned where it is sheltered from autumn winds. There are also several so-called
'snake-bark' maples which originated in China, including *A.
davidii* and its subspecies *grosseri*, but these are bigger and
more bulky than the paper-bark maple, as well as being less

spectacular in the autumn. This is another tree that does not require pruning.

Pagoda tree (Taa-Muh) *Sophora japonica* 'Pendula'
Element: *Yang*
Symbolism: *Stability/learning*
The deciduous *S. japonica* is occasionally also referred to as the 'scholar tree' by Feng Shui gardeners who believe it represents stability and learning. The variety 'Pendula' has been a favourite in the great Peking gardens for centuries, where its stiffly drooping branches, known as 'dragon claws', form natural arbours. The pagoda tree is distinguished by its branches which spread out from about 2–3m up the trunk and are said to be ideal conductors of *Chi*. It is slow growing but very vigorous, and can last a lifetime and more. It has dark green leaves turning yellow in autumn, rare tiny white, pea-like flowers (which only appear on the trees after they are 30 years old and then in high summer) and a brown bark with rather willow-like ridges. The tree can be planted in March or April in any fertile, well-drained soil in a sunny position that is sheltered from north and east winds. Seeds may be sown at the same time in a cold frame or greenhouse, and when they are large enough should be allowed to grow for another three years before being transplanted to their final location at any time between October and March. Feng Shui says the *Chi* attraction of the pagoda tree is such that it makes an ideal tree to sit by for reflection and study.

Laceback pine (Sung) *Pinus bungeana*
Element: *Yang*
Symbolism: *Nobility*
This species of pine is said by Feng Shui to represent nobility and integrity—nobility because it has always been associated with rulers, and integrity because it does not wither in the winter and remains faithful in adversity. The writer Li Li-weng once compared a garden without an aged pine to a group of pretty women without a man to set them off! The laceback pine has the ability to endure the cold and

generally has a low, often bushy shape which can used in landscaping (especially by a rock garden), or as a shelter tree in a small to medium garden. It came originally from north-west China, grows to around 10–15m (30–50ft) with a spread of 5–6m (15–20ft), and has dark green needles in groups of three, dull yellow flowers, and brown, egg-shaped cones about 5–7cm (2–3ins) long. The bark is unique— smooth grey-green and olive brown, flaking away to leave white patches which turn successively yellow, pale green, olive, rufous, purple and purple-brown—the shades of integrity, according to Feng Shui. Seeds can be sown in March, with the seedlings being planted out the following spring where they should be allowed to grow for two or three years before being transplanted to their final position. Although the lacebark pine is not easy to establish in the West, it is another of the Feng Shui trees that is well worth cherishing for the energy it can bring to the garden. The larger species of pine are, of course, found in almost all forest areas of the world, but with heights up to 40m (130ft) are hardly ideal for the average garden.

Rowan (Juhurng) *Sorbus hupehensis*
Element: *Yin*
Symbolism: *Youth*
Sometimes called the Hubei Rowan after the area of Western China where it was first recorded, this tree is noted for being sturdy and upright when young—the characteristics all young people should strive for, according to Feng Shui. It also says that the tree's groups of pendulous silvery grey-green leaves which turn red from October onwards, and the clusters of flowers with their narrow-stalked petals, yellow centre and purple anthers are good conductors of *Chi*. *S. hupehensis* grows to a height and spread of 8m (25ft). Like any rowan, this species can be planted in an ordinary, well-drained site between October and March. Seeds, on the other hand, can be extracted from the berries in October and sown in a cold frame for three to five years before finally being located during the autumn.

Silk tree (Rurnghua-Shuh) *Albizia julibrissin rosea*
Element: *Yin*
Symbolism: *Industry*
Although it has no connection with the making of silk—silk worms actually feed on the leaves of white mulberry trees—*A. julibrissin rosea* produces silky pink flower plumes that look rather like powderpuffs and can give a garden quite an exotic effect when they are in bloom. Feng Shui says the resemblance with silk means that the tree is symbolic of the industry of silkworms and will be of particular inspiration to those who work at home. The plumes of flowers and the feathery, fernlike mid-green leaves, each with its overlapping leaflets, are good conductors of *Chi*. The tree can grow up to 6m (20ft) high, but with its spreading canopy allows sunlight through so that it will not kill off grass if positioned as a lawn specimen. It can be planted in March in full sun and has no problem growing in poor soil. However, seeds will require at least a year's growth under glass before the shoots are ready for the garden. Feng Shui says that the silk tree can be used to create a fine shading for a patio and will also ensure the smooth flow of energy into a house or flat.

Tree of heaven (Tian-Muh) *Ailanthus altissima*
Element: *Yang*
Symbolism: *Protection*
Although the average person in the UK may not be aware of the fact, the exotically named 'tree of heaven' is found in many London squares, streets and parks and is also common enough in gardens in the southern half of England. Originating from northern China, the tree has a long history of fulfilling its ancient Feng Shui role of protecting buildings from bad *Sha*. With its strongly ascending branches bearing a tall, irregular dome and bright, deep-red leaves which unfold in mid-June, *A. altissima* can survive city pollution and bad weather. The young trees have smooth, grey-brown bark, patterned with white angular streaks, which turn to a dark grey with dark streaks scaling very finely as it ages. It

is a tree that grows quickly, can be planted in the autumn, and may reach heights of up to 25m (80ft). The tree of heaven will also make the best of a thin soil because its roots can stretch a considerable distance, sometimes throwing up a root-sucker some distance from the bole. A similar, though rarer, species is the downy tree of heaven, *A. vilmoriniana*, which comes from western China and has darker leaves with deep red rachis.

Tulip tree (Yuhjin) *Liriodendron chinense*
Element: *Yang*
Symbolism: *Grandeur*
The tulip tree is, with a height of 25m (80ft) and spread of 12m (40ft), is too big for the average Western garden, but in Central China where it was first discovered, it was recognised as a handsome, rapidly growing tree which would enhance a garden by its grandeur. The dark green, saddle-shaped leaves unfold brown in May and turn bright yellow in the autumn. It is not until the tree is 15 years old that the cup-shaped flowers start to appear in mid-July—they are green with yellow veins and about 50 stamens. The tulip tree is said to be an ideal conductor of *Chi*, but a Western gardener seeking one for his garden would have to order the species from a specialist nursery. It should be planted in spring in a well-drained, sunny position.

Weeping willow (Chueir-Lioou) *Salix babylonica*
Element: *Yin*
Symbolism: *Grace*
The weeping willow is one of the most famous trees in the world, as well as being regarded by Feng Shui as perhaps the finest of all conductors of *Chi* in a garden. Long considered the 'Emblem of Spring' in China (where it is sometimes simply referred to as *Liu*), it was given its curious botanical name, *S. babylonica*, by Carl Linnaeus in the eighteenth century under the mistaken impression that he was dealing with the tree referred to in Psalm 137 as a willow which stood by the waters of Babylon. The leaves, root and

bark, and the gum which exudes from the tree, have all been used in medicine by the Chinese, while the thin branches have been made into ropes and baskets. In Feng Shui it is said to be a 'herb of immortality' because of its ability to grow from the smallest branch stuck in the earth. In antiquity, the willow was believed to have supernatural powers, and it is known that during the T'ang dynasty the rebel leader Huang Ch'ao, who sacked the city of Ch'ang-an, spared all those families who had hung willow branches over their doors. The supple grace of the willow branches drew comparisons with the waists of dancing girls, and this was later used to suggest sexual freedom and prostitution. For this reason, many Chinese would not plant a willow at the rear of their gardens where the women's rooms were situated. Subsequently in the West, the healing powers of the tree led to the manufacture of aspirin, a chemically produced version of the pain-killer it contains.

Growing to a height and spread of 12m (40ft) the willow gets its familiar name from the slender pale to mid-green leaves which appear in spring, clinging to the sinuous curves of the brown branches, and remain to provide delight until well into autumn. The fluffy, cylindrical catkins are silvery green but later turn yellow with pollen as the stamens expand. Although often found beside rivers and park ponds, the weeping willow will grow equally well in dry or damp soil and can be planted from cuttings in the autumn or early spring, though well away from any buildings. A hybrid, *S.× sepulcralis* 'Chrysocoma', is very similar to this variety but with golden leaves. Some gardening experts argue that it grows better and is less subject to canker than the original Chinese tree.

ORNAMENTAL FRUIT TREES

Almond (Shihngrern) *Prunus dulcis*
Element: *Yin*
Symbolism: *Good luck*
The earliest wild almond tree, *Prunus triloba*, with its single pink flowers and green fruit covered in dense hairs containing the familiar brown nut, was known to the Chinese many centuries ago. It became symbolic of good luck because of the nutritional qualities of the nut, but in northern Europe and Britain the tree is grown mainly as an ornament: in the colder climate it rarely produces good-quality nuts. The common almond, *P. dulcis*, has a height and spread of about 8m (25ft) and grows vigorously. It has a nearly black bark, deeply cracked, rather dull green leaves but large clear pink flowers which cluster along the naked branches in March and April. The almond can be grown from seed, but a cultivated plant layered in spring is more likely to be the choice of someone living in a city or suburban area where the tree has become a familiar sight in the last half-century. A Chinese version, *P. glandulosa*, is much smaller at 1.5m (5ft), but with its bushy shape, slender shoots and white or pink flowers, can enhance the Feng Shui of a garden by being planted beside a lawn or rock garden.

Crab apple (Shaguoo) *Malus spectabilis*
Element: *Yang*
Symbolism: *Splendour*
The Chinese crab apple tree is recognised as the parent of many of the edible apples we enjoy today. Although most frequently grown now for decoration, crab apples can also be used for making preserves and in their native land are still sometimes cooked with meat, vegetables and in fruit dishes. In the West the crab apple is more often seen as a beautiful focal point in the heart of a garden, and this is very good Feng Shui if the tree is correctly positioned according to the Five Animals. It will enhance the flow of the *Chi* around the whole garden, as well as providing a calm and

romantic spot. The Chinese crab apple, true to its botanical name and symbolism, looks splendid with its twisting, drooping branches covered in rosy-pink buds opening to blush-pink semi-double, slightly fragrant flowers which appear in mid-spring. These are followed by the yellowish fruits flushed with red which ripen in September and October. This particular species can grow to as much as 10m (30ft) high, which makes it unsuitable for a small city garden.

All crab apple trees are among the hardiest and easiest to grow of flowering trees; they are best in a sunny position in well-drained soil. They can be planted from October to March and benefit from an annual mulch in April. Although crab apples can be grown from seed, they usually take up to ten years to reach flowering size. Centuries ago, Feng Shui experts decided that, given room and space, the crab apple was one of the most important trees for a garden; the ancient art also said that where space permitted a small grove of crab apple trees of different species, consisting of the white, pink and red flowering kinds, created excellent *Chi* and a very relaxing and harmonious environment.

Apricot (Shihng) *Prunus armeniaca*
Element: *Yin*
Symbolism: *Fruitfulness*
According to legend, the Chinese once made a medicine called 'Apricot Gold' which was said to extend the lifespan to seven hundred years! It is described in a volume entitled *Pent 'Sao*, and consists of the double kernels of the fruit gathered from trees growing in 'auspicious places'—in other words, sites that had been declared favourable by Feng Shui. Today we know that apricots are good for anaemia (because they contain a small percentage of copper), and the fresh fruits contain such valuable mineral salts as phosphorus and silica. Many liqueurs have been derived from the kernel of the apricot, and the Chinese often use the oil from the fruit as a substitute for almond oil. The leaves can be dried to mix with tea, or used by themselves to relieve a cough; while Oriental ladies use the flowers in many of their cos-

metics. The petals are also claimed to have aphrodisiac qualities. Although its botanical name suggests that apricots originated in Armenia, they are actually believed to have first been found in Shansi where there are many legends about the tree. Confucius is said to have chosen a grove of apricots in which to write many of his works. Feng Shui warns that the apricot tree should never be planted on a south-facing wall because if it flowers too early it may well fall victim to the first frost—an east or west wall is best.

The trees grow to about 3m (10ft) with a similar spread, and should be planted during October or November in any fertile, well-drained soil. To obtain a fan-trained tree, it will require holding with wires against a warm, sheltered wall, with perhaps a little pruning when the desired height and shape are achieved. The clusters of white flowers, sometimes flushed pink, appear from February to March, to be followed in August by the familiar yellow fruit, faintly tinged with red. The golden colour and symbolism of fruitfulness has made the apricot an important tree in Feng Shui gardening, although it must be admitted that in Britain it is only in the warmer parts of southern England that reliable cropping can be expected.

Wild cherry (Yingtaur) *Prunus avium*
Element: *Yang*
Symbolism: *Contentment*
This species of cherry is also known as the gean, and in China Feng Shui has regarded it since the very earliest times as having the ability to create harmony between the mind and body and produce a good disposition. With its vigorous growth, generally globe-like shape and pendant flowers and berries, *P. avium* is an excellent conductor of *Chi* and was the parent of most of the sweet cherries we eat today. The tree can grow to about 20m (70ft) with a spread of about 10m (30ft). The leaves and flowers open together in April, with the cherries turning from glossy yellow to bright red by July—when, of course, they become a favourite target for

birds. Chinese experts say the trees are best propagated from seeds as they are generally longer lived, but heel cuttings can be planted in a cold frame in August or September and planted out the following spring. The cherry does not require regular pruning, but to retain a good rounded shape a branch or two may have to be removed in late summer.

Two other ornamental Chinese cherries which are recommended by Feng Shui are *P. conradinea* which flowers early with fragrant white or pink flowers, and *P. serrula* which has narrow, rather willow-like leaves, pretty white flowers and a most striking bark which peels off in strips to reveal polished red-brown new bark beneath. There is no doubt that the cherry is one of the beauties of spring, its flowers a source of inspiration after the bleakness of winter. In China, where the fruit is eaten, used as a medicine and made into a drink, it is said to prevent the 'loss of vision'.

Peach (Taur) *Prunus persica*
Element: *Yang*
Symbolism: *Immortality*
In Chinese lore and legend the peach is said to embody fecundity and immortality, while in Feng Shui it is held to be a symbol of spring, marriage and, again, immortality. There is a story told that a peach growing in the garden of Hsi Wang Mu, the Taoist's Mother Goddess of the West, was said to ripen every three thousand years and its fruits conferred eternal life on those who ate them. Feng Shui claims that the pale pink flowers of *P. persica* have the power to drive away evil *Sha*, although it insists that it is a back garden tree and should never be grown at the front of a house. In China it is also said that the kernels of the fruit are good for stomach complaints and the milk extracted from them will induce sleep and cure headaches if rubbed on the forehead. Confucius was just one among many of his countrymen who believed that this tree sent out a symbolic message to all those who viewed it: 'Your qualities, like your charms, are unequalled.'

Growing to a height and spread of 8m (25ft), the ornamental peach opens its flowers in April and the yellow-golden fruits ripen from July onwards. It can be grown from seed, though not easily, and it is better as a young plant introduced in the spring, ideally placed against a sunny wall. Another species from China, *P. davidiana*, may grow somewhat bigger, and although its single, white or rose-coloured flowers can open as early as January, it must be placed in a sheltered setting. Feng Shui says this species is particularly beneficial if grown against a dark background or corner as the bright flowers will deflect any bad *Sha* that might collect there.

Callery pear (Tzyy) *Pyrus calleryana*
Element: *Yin*
Symbolism: *Longevity*
The pear is also associated with longevity—although less so than the peach—because specimens have been known to live for as long as 300 years. Along with the peach and plum, the tree has been grown in China more for its blossoms than its fruit, and because the famous Duke of Shao, renowned for his impartiality, always sat beneath one when administering justice, it has also become symbolic of good government. The callery pear is a beautiful, inverted bowl-shaped tree which bursts into a mass of heavy white flowers in the spring, following this display in the autumn by turning its glossy dark green leaves into a lustrous purple colour that has been popular in Feng Shui ever since it was first discovered in northern China. Its gorgeous appearance, however, should not be allowed to detract from the fact that this is a hardy tree which can live happily in the most polluted city streets.

The bloom of the callery pear has been described as resembling that of the crab apple, and it is certainly not a good idea to have both in one garden. *P. calleryana*, for its part, can provide an attractive lawn feature for most of the year. It grows to a height and spread of 15m (50ft) and should be propagated from cuttings in a sunny spot. It can adapt to most well-drained soil conditions but is unsuitable for small gardens. The pears develop in the autumn in clusters of small, round, brown fruits. Most of the modern edible pear tree varieties developed from another species, *P. communis*, which is found from the Himalayas to S. W. Asia. One of its offspring, the sweet and juicy 'Conference' pear which can be picked in September for eating in October, has a tapering shape which Feng Shui says is a good conductor of *Chi*.

Plum (Lan Hua) *Prunus mume*
Element: *Yang*
Symbolism: *Vitality*
The exquisitely scented *lan hua* has been popular with the Chinese since antiquity and because it divided into two main classes—spring and autumn blooming—and had strangely varied petals, it became an object of competition among growers. For generations in Shanghai, shows were held twice a year which attracted hundreds of competitors to pit their finest blooms against one another. In Feng Shui the plum is said to promise spring and the renewal of vitality and hope, and the *Chi* of a garden can be enhanced by placing one near a water feature; for years the Chinese used to cast the petals of plum flowers onto their rivers in the hope of attracting wealth and good fortune. The ancient art says that this tree is best planted on a raised bed (known as a *t'ai* in China) with a little stone wall as edging.

 P. mume is a small tree with rounded, mid-green leaves and clusters of pale pink flowers that grow along its slender branches in late winter or early spring and can sometimes be in full bloom as early as February. It is a shallow-rooting tree and the soil around it should not be cultivated too often or too deeply. Planting is best done in early autumn, but when the weather is mild this can be undertaken during the winter right up until March. The ornamental plum likes well-drained soil, preferably with a trace of lime. It can be propagated from cuttings or seeds and seed-raised trees are said to be longer-lived. Pruning is not generally necessary to keep the tree in good shape for conducting the *Chi*, but if grown purely for flowering, then trim after this is over and cut back the old flowering shoots. For the small garden of a ground-floor flat or apartment, the ornamental plum combines beauty, fragrance and good Feng Shui in equal measure.

7 *THE STRENGTH OF BAMBOO*

One of the most versatile and effective plants you can employ in enhancing the Feng Shui of a garden is bamboo, which has been a staple in Chinese life since the very earliest times. Yet despite its association with the East and tropical climates in general, the bamboo cane may be grown quite easily in the milder climates of the West and put to use in a variety of ways, from decorative purposes to plant support and as an ideal screening material.

In China, the bamboo, or *baumuh*, is traditionally known as one of the 'Three Friends of Winter'—the other two are the pine tree and apricot which can also bloom on bare branches even in the snow—and has a strong *Yang* quality. This strength is reflected in an old Chinese saying, 'The palace has arisen firm as the roots of a clump of bamboo', and Confucius saw the plant, bending in the wind but never breaking, as a symbol of the true gentleman. The famous Emperor Ch'ien-lung claimed that the sight of bamboo made him think of virtue. It is no surprise, therefore, to learn that bamboo has been used by the Chinese for centuries as a means of protection against evil spirits and inclement elements. Early on, too, Feng Shui devised a fence of *baumuh* canes with a circular bowl of matted bamboo leaves which, when raised on a pole over the garden wall, would keep any bad *Sha* away from a property (see p. 122).

Widely regarded by the people of China as a 'servant of all work', the bamboo has been utilised as the framework for houses, in the making of beds, tables, chairs and cupboards, as well as hundreds of other small household items. It can be worn, eaten and used as medicine. Shavings of the plant had been taken to stuff pillows and mattresses, while the canes have been used in all manner of items from containers to cages for pets, including stands for flowers and even tools for gardening.

According to Chinese tradition, there is a substance to be found in the cavities between the knots of certain bamboos (especially the *Melocanna bambusoides*) which consists of silica and a little lime and vegetable. This is used to make the famous Chinese medicine, *Tabashir*, which it is claimed can heal any ailment. An old superstition says that, should the rarely occurring flowering of the bamboo take place, it is an omen of disaster—and that was certainly the case in Hong Kong just prior to the terrible plague which ravaged the country in 1894. Shortly after this followed the disastrous Sino-Japanese war. Of all the plant's remarkable qualities, A. B. Freeman-Mitford has written in his study, *The Bamboo*

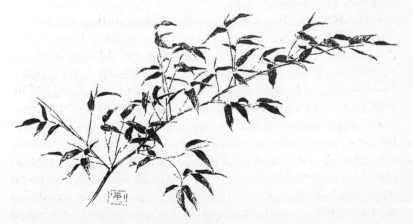

The increasingly popular black-stemmed bamboo, *Phyllostachys nigra*, provides excellent Feng Shui for the smaller garden.

Garden (1896), 'House, furniture, art, clothes, arms, food and medicine, what does this wonderful plant not supply— and it is all so cheap, too!'

The group of plants known as bamboo belongs to the family of woody perennial grasses called Gramineae. They are remarkable for the enormous variety of circumferences and sizes to which they can grow, from quite small to enormous. The rounded stems are hollow and jointed, with colours from the lightest shade of yellow to a very deep black. Today, China still leads the world in the production of those garden canes which have become such an essential in gardening. Just to the north-west of Canton there is an area of land of over one hundred square miles which is completely given over to the cultivation of a species of bamboo known as *Pseudosasa amabilis.* It is here that more than 80 per cent of the world's garden canes are produced. These canes take three years to mature, but are sometimes cut after two years to meet demand. When buying canes from a garden centre it is as well to try to establish their age, or at least to feel the bamboos carefully, for the younger ones are often still weak and may bend when first put to use.

The bamboo is found in almost as many different varieties as it has shapes and sizes. Those of the genus known as *Phyllostachys* are, however, generally considered the most suitable for growing in the West—either from seed, cutting or division—as they flourish more strongly in our climate than the *Fargesia* genus which are very susceptible to changes in the weather. The most famous example of this is *Fargesia murieliae,* the umbrella bamboo, with its spray of 4m (12ft) high green stems, which had for years been recommended by gardening experts until just recently, when examples all over the world mysteriously flowered and died. This led to a natural reluctance among growers to plant them. However, this is all very much to our advantage, as the *Phyllostachys* are the more striking and ornamental of the two types and in Feng Shui philosophy are believed to be superior. Here are the half-dozen most popular species recommended by the ancient art, which gardeners might like to consider growing from either seed or plant:

Phyllostachys aureosulcata 'Spectabilis'
This is an instantly recognisable and very hardy species. The stems are yellow with a striking green stripe running down between the joints on alternate sides of the plant. The yellow turns orange when the bamboo is in full sun. This species is very popular with gardeners who enjoy flower arranging as it can form the ideal accompaniment to a whole range of blooms.

Phyllostachys bambusoides 'Castilloni'
Another, slightly deeper yellow, species which also has a green stripe between alternate joints. The drawback to 'Castilloni' is that it has proved less hardy than 'Spectabilis' and the new shoots are vulnerable to frost in the spring.

Phyllostachys propinqua
A fast-growing species with chunky stems and leaves in a rich, glossy green. This plant is ideal for creating a natural effect when several are grown together. *P. propinqua* can grow to over 4m (12ft) in three years and at its optimum can double that size.

Phyllostachys nigra
This is the famous and increasingly popular black-stemmed bamboo which Feng Shui says is absolutely ideal for the small garden. It grows in little clumps to about 4m (12ft) high and never becomes invasive. *P. nigra* should be placed in full sun to ensure that its initially pale stems turn black. The colour actually deepens as the plant matures, and as it grows it is a good idea to snip off the older, outer stems to allow the sunlight to blacken those inside.

Thamnocalamus crassinodus
A species of bamboo at the other end of the spectrum, with
alternate white and light green stems between the joints. *T.
crassinodus* is a very straight and sturdy variety which can
grow to more than 3m (10ft) high and is, I am told, a favourite with a number of European landscape gardeners.

Chusquea breviglumis
A stolid, deep-green species with fat stems, which is ideal for
planting in a thicket or grove. Feng Shui experts say the *C.
breviglumis* is ready-made for planting alongside a meandering path as the plants will readily assist the *Chi* to circulate
throughout the garden.

Because most bamboos grow quickly, they can have the dual
effect of enhancing the beauty of a garden while they grow,
and then being put to practical use when mature. It has
been estimated, for example, that a hectare of land can
produce between 10 to 25 tonnes of bamboo wood per year.
But as quality rather than quantity is our objective in this
book, let us just consider growing a few plants as part of the
landscape of a Feng Shui garden.

Baumuh can be grown quite satisfactorily from seed and
should be sown when the seeds are very hard. August is the
ideal month to put them out in a tray in the garden. The
seedlings will then germinate almost before your eyes! (If
you fancy eating the shoots, cut them as soon as they
emerge—once above ground the little stems soon become
woody.)

When selecting a location in which to plant bamboo, find
somewhere protected from the wind as the foliage can be
damaged by bad weather, especially in the winter. While the
plants are still young they should be watered regularly as
they will die if allowed to dry out. In fact, only when bamboo
is fully established can it survive a drought.

Bamboo also benefits from being fed well early in the
season. Do not continue this too long or you will generate
tender, late growth which can easily be damaged by winter

frosts. The quality of the plant can be improved by a good mulch in the spring when the new shoots are sprouting.

It is also as well to be aware that the first stems of the bamboo may look droopy. Do not be tempted to remove these for the canes only get fatter and taller as the plant matures. If, the following year, the majority of the canes are upright and tall, the earlier, bent stems can be clipped off.

Finally, when growing bamboo remember that it is not a native of these shores. It may well prove slow to establish itself in your garden, especially if you do not have the rich loamy soil it enjoys. If in any doubt, it is well worth buying a plant which is already a year or two old. This already possesses the energy to thrive just as it once did in the harshest corners of China.

If you have neither the space nor the inclination to grow bamboo, there is no reason why you should not purchase canes from a local supplier to use in building the kind of items that will help the Feng Shui of your garden, such as trellises, screens and perhaps even a loggia.

Although there exists an old European illustration of trelliswork which dates back to the fourteenth century— showing two lovers in a garden surrounded by a low, diagonally trellised fence covered by climbing roses—the Chinese were actually using free-standing constructions to support their roses at least two centuries earlier. Today, in the West, we regard the high point of trellismaking as the late seventeenth and early eighteenth centuries when the art of *treillage* was developed in France. this style of floral presentation, with its ingenious use of alcoves, archways and doors, was most often seen in the gardens of the great *châteaux*—particularly at Versailles—but nevertheless the tradition has survived, albeit rather less grandly, and can now be regarded as one of the most pleasant ways of transforming a small garden or altering its perspective.

Feng Shui reached this conclusion much earlier— although it did not use trellis to contain or formalise the growth of roses or any other climbing plants, but to allow them to meander naturally and facilitate the smooth flow of

A trellis of bamboo canes is very effective in protecting a house and garden from bad *Sha*, as this sketch of a Chinese building shows.

Chi. Bamboo canes can also be used to create compartments or perhaps a screen around a patio, providing the garden with the illusion of increased size as well as extra privacy. This is good Feng Shui, so long as the construction details are to the rear to give the impression of a continuous and undulating expanse of *baumuh* over which the *Chi* can pass. Do bear this in mind when positioning a trellis in your own garden, and don't ignore the fact that bamboo has several advantages over the ready-made, often poor-quality timber or unattractive plastic trellis panelling that is generally available.

In several gardens in the West I have seen bamboo con-

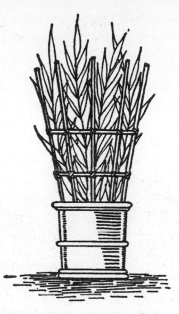

Bamboo canes used as supports for pot plants – even for young bamboo shoots! – will enhance the Feng Shui of gardens of all sizes.

structions which were simple to erect and provided the necessary support for climbing plants. All of them utilised narrow bamboo canes bound together to form a diagonally-patterned trellis. In two cases the walls behind the bamboo frames had been painted white to afford an attractive back-drop to good Feng Shui flowers like roses and wisteria, while in front of them grew a number of other energy-makers, including asters and chrysanthemums. One trellis I saw even had a little clump of black bamboo, *Phyllostachys nigra*, sited right alongside it, apparently doubling its *Chi* efficiency.

Lastly, if you have a very small garden indeed, bamboos make excellent pot plants, and the canes can be used to form attractive supports for other flowers growing in containers as the example illustrated here shows. Bamboo plants look very distinctive when grown in big Chinese ceramic pots—and when carefully positioned in relationship to your door or windows can be efficient channels for the *Chi*. And another advantage of growing bamboos in a container is that they do not invade the whole garden as they are very prone to do if not carefully watched.

8 POOLS OF DELIGHT

Ponds and rockeries can lend enchantment to any garden, and are two more features of modern gardening that we owe to the philosophy of Feng Shui and the experiments of Chinese gardeners many years ago. The pond evolved from the fact that water is a vital element in human life, while the rockery or rock garden came as a direct result of the people's love of mountains, with their perceived symbolism of protection and security. Both features are also considered important channels of a garden's earth energies, the *Chi*. The expression 'digging ponds and piling mountains' has been synonymous in China for many years with the making of gardens.

The English historian H. N. Wethered sensed something of this enchantment when he wrote of China in his *A Short History of Gardens* (1933), 'The people divert streams through their gardens, creating miniature waterfalls, and excavate soil for artificial pools to invite the spirits of the wind, the air and the water ... Mountains in the Chinese mind also attract a peculiar reverence as exerting a propitious influence on human life; and mountains in a garden, if only the size of molehills, have a symbolic meaning pointing to good fortune ...'

A Chinese writer, Yang Hung-hsien, has gone a step farther in his delightful philosophical work, *Wen Wu* (1957): 'It is water above all that creates the mild, congenial and yet lively atmosphere which, since it best revives the spirit, is the ultimate purpose of a garden. Nothing else produces quite the same serene effect as a pool where a visitor stands alone in opposition to space and is divinely delighted with its pure expanse.'

The very meaning of the words 'Feng Shui'—wind and water—are a clear indication of their importance in the ancient art, and particularly so in the garden. Indeed, it is not without significance that when the Chinese word for *Chi* is spoken it bears a distinct similarity to that for 'stream'. Rocks for their part are seen to be as different from water as *Yin* is from *Yang*, although both are inextricably linked together and require each other to generate balance and harmony.

The wise men who were responsible for defining the powers of Feng Shui reached one of their most important conclusions by observing the elements all around them, especially the wind and water. It seemed clear to them that the manner in which smoke was carried on the breeze and water ebbed and flowed along a river was how *Chi* circulated throughout the environment. Modern science now accepts that this study enabled the Chinese to understand the working of convection currents long before this branch of physics had become a scientific fact in the West.

Feng Shui says that rivers, streams, lakes, pools and even small ponds—all forms of watercourses, in fact—are potentially good conductors of *Chi*. But what is very important is *how* the water flows. A river that meanders naturally across the countryside, or a lake that forms its own curved shoreline, is better able to direct the flow of the natural energies than a watercourse which runs in a straight line or has sharp bends, because these allow the precious *Chi* to 'run off' and dissipate.

In the West there has been a tendency among water authorities to straighten rivers and drainage channels. The policy in

A water feature has always been considered a very important element in the Feng Shui of gardens, whatever their size.

China, by contrast, is to encourage the water to follow a more natural course, even in the irrigating of rice fields. I recently saw a prime example of this Feng Shui at work in what was formerly the British colony of Hong Kong. There I came across a number of what had once been straight waterways curved and diverted to form horseshoe-shaped moats. These bends, I was told, had enhanced the flow of *Chi* as well as improving the quality of the local agricultural land.

The Chinese also believe that water is symbolic of wealth and rank. This is another reason why a gently flowing stream has the advantage over one that moves quickly, for it will conserve the *Chi* in the locality instead of carrying it away. And a stretch of water that meanders around a property is said to ensure a steady flow of good fortune to the inhabitants. In London, the opening up of Docklands for residential property along the bends of the Thames has made this a particularly auspicious area and much sought-after by those who believe in the ways of Feng Shui. (Incidentally, according to the ancient art, a watercourse which approaches a property directly from the east or west is said to be more propitious than one from the north or south.)

By tradition, water should always flow past the front of a building. In China, where this did not occur naturally it became standard practice for property owners to build ornamental pools before their front entrances. Where this was not possible, Feng Shui allowed for the introduction of a water feature either at the front or rear . . . so long as it curved in the direction of the house. This was said to give the impression that the pool was embracing the home and directing good *Chi* towards it. On no account, however, should a pool be designed to curve *away* from a building, as this would generate bad *Sha*.

That garden pools were being built in China long before the idea had reached the West can be gathered from the account of Marco Polo of an ornamental pond in the palace gardens of Kublai Khan at Cambaluc, which he saw during his travels (1271–95). Indeed, he refers to several stretches of water overshadowed by rocks which resembled miniature mountains, standing in the gardens of rich merchants. Beside these were earthenware vessels planted with flowers, including bamboos, azaleas and hydrangeas, as well as a wooden bench on which the owner could sit and contemplate the changing vistas of the skies and the reflection of his surroundings in the water.

The whole purpose of these pools was to represent the great lake views of an ideal Feng Shui site. No matter how shallow they were, they created an impression of depth and distance, as well as reflecting the buildings and ensuring the circulation of the *Chi*.

Feng Shui says that the energy quotient of a garden pond can be improved by stocking it with fish or even a terrapin. Gold and silver fish are especially recommended—they symbolise valuable coins—and for centuries many Chinese have kept hardy terrapins beside their water features. The terrapin, being a cold-blooded reptile, can survive long periods in water and is believed to be symbolic of long life and stability; keeping one is said to enhance the owner's chances of enjoying the same good fortune.

Another old Chinese proverb says that a garden without water is like a body without life-blood. Feng Shui goes farther, stating that it is not sufficient to have a still pond, because one that is activated by a fountain or mechanical pump will better aid the movement of the *Chi.* Running water will improve the environment and also cancel out negative influences such as everyday noise and passing traffic. It symbolises the flow of money, too, and can be very beneficial to a property where a business is being carried on.

Here are a few tips on making a garden pond that will possess its quota of visual magic, attract wildlife including birds, dragonflies and frogs, and meet the requirements of Feng Shui.

The easiest way to construct such a pond is to use a butyl rubber liner, because it is tough, long-lasting and flexible and comes in almost any size. This will allow you to decide upon your own shape, and ideally, following the guidelines of Feng Shui, opt for a kidney shape like the *Yin* or *Yang* symbol which is a good conductor of *Chi.* An alternative shape might be a rectangle resembling the Chinese character *kou* which means a mouth and symbolises people and posterity. To establish what size of liner you need, mark out the shape and measure the maximum length and width, then add twice the maximum depth to each of these measurements and a further 30cm (12ins) for the overlap at the edges. Purchase your liner before beginning work.

Once you have selected a suitable site for the pond—which should be on sunny, level ground away from any overhanging trees—mark out the shape again with string and pegs or, better still, a hosepipe, and cut all round this. Lift the turf with a spade and dig out the pond so that the centre is at least 60cm (2ft) deep. Outside the marker at ground level remove the turf all round to a width of 45cm (18ins) and a depth of 5cm (2ins), to create a ledge where marginal plants can be grown. Next clear away any sharp stones or debris from the bottom of the hole and cover the whole base with a layer of fine sand to a depth of about 2.5cm (1in).

Now spread the liner across the bottom and over the sides of the hole and secure the edges with bricks. Once you are satisfied the liner is in the position you require—and it might not be a bad idea to allow it several hours in the sun to settle—fill the pond *slowly*. This will allow the weight of the water to stretch the rubber gently into shape and should be continued until the water level is about 5cm (2ins) from the top. Once the pond is full, remove the bricks and place some suitable large stones or ornamental flagstones to cover the liner, or tuck the edges under the surrounding turf.

No pool would be complete without a few aquatic plants, and Feng Shui especially recommends water lilies such as *Nymphaea odorata* 'Sulphurea Grandiflora' with their lucky yellow flowers. For the margins a group of *Pontederia cordata* or some vigorous yellow flag iris can hardly be bettered, while the water can be kept clear by adding a few sprigs of *Lagarosiphon major*. The ultimate choice for a pond would obviously be some lotus flowers (*Nelumbo nucifera*) growing in pots, but they do need a warm situation and a conservatory or greenhouse to survive the winter. One Feng Shui gardener I talked to recommended the use of special planting baskets filled with aquatic compost for any aquatic plants in a pond. He also suggested a layer of water-washed gravel for submerged plants to root into.

Leave the pond and plants to settle down and establish for a few weeks, which will also allow the oxygen level to stabilise. Then the whole effect should be completed with the addition of some goldfish.

Or almost completed, I should say, for the gardener added

that such a pond should always have moving water to ensure good Feng Shui. His suggestion was to place a large wedge of granite in the middle of the pond with a small stone saucer fixed to the top, serving as a water bowl. Next thread a copper pipe through a bamboo spout and link this to a small submersible electric pump situated near the base of the granite. This enables the water to be circulated from the pool into the bowl and, as it overflows and runs back into the pond, creates the delightful sound of gently splashing water. The novice gardener will probably require some specialist help in installing this feature, *especially where any electrical wiring is concerned*, but the end result will certainly generate some very good *Chi* for the garden.

Many Feng Shui gardeners also believe that a miniature pagoda, modelled on traditional Chinese lines, is a good accompaniment to a water feature. The original pagodas were raised by the Chinese to improve the *Chi* quality of their lands and especially to ensure better crops. The models, which can range from little mushroom-shaped versions just a few centimetres high to multi-storied edifices of a metre or more, are best placed on the bank of the pond or adjacent to a rockery. In China, most contemporary model pagodas are made of porcelain, although some of the bigger versions based on classic examples are constructed of thin, lightweight boards attached to a framework of bamboo. By and large, they are less grandiose and vividly painted than the pagodas which the Japanese have copied for their gardens. The most favoured direction for a model pagoda to face is the south-west.

A garden that is too small for a pond can still have a water feature. A wooden half-barrel or a stone trough are both recommended by Feng Shui because of their association with the Five Elements. Either might be incorporated into a patio, and then made all the more attractive by planting a flowering plant or two on the margins. Even a miniature fountain could be added to generate that wonderfully soothing and therapeutic sound that is always provided by splashing water.

Miniature pagodas of all shapes and sizes used in conjunction with water features have been part of Feng Shui practice for centuries.

Now let us turn our attention to the rockery. In general terms, Feng Shui believes that rockeries are best situated in the north and west of a garden, as a shield for the pond which ideally lies to the south and east. Try to avoid the reverse situation as these positions are not propitious for either feature.

To modern eyes, the early Chinese rock gardens would have looked bizarre indeed. In those days, the people favoured massive grey stones which invariably dominated a garden and were intended to provide a buffer against the elements in much the same way as a real hill or mountain does for the landscape in its lee. The Chinese word for 'landscape' is *shan shui* which literally means 'mountains and water', and the combination is said to evoke the ancient 'Isles of the Immortals'. Legend has it that anyone who reached this holy place and conversed with the immortals would perhaps gain the secret of eternal life. Chinese history records that a number of the great rulers of China—in particular the Han Emperor, Wu-ti—tried to lure these immortals down to earth by building huge rocky islands and lakes that were a mirror image of their sacred dwelling-place.

For centuries stones were virtually objects of reverence to the Chinese because of their importance in *Yin* and *Yang*. In the eleventh and twelfth centuries, for example, there was an explosion of rock-worship (or petromania), when rival noblemen literally fought over the finest examples with their extraordinary furrows, holes, bumps and craggy edges. The Emperor Hui-tsung's collection apparently became so large that it almost crippled the nation financially.

According to Feng Shui, stones represent the stillness of rocks in partnership with flowing streams, masculine strength with feminine moisture, and the juxtaposition of the rough with the smooth. This association takes on an even deeper significance in relation to another ancient Chinese belief that rivers are the earth's arteries and moun-

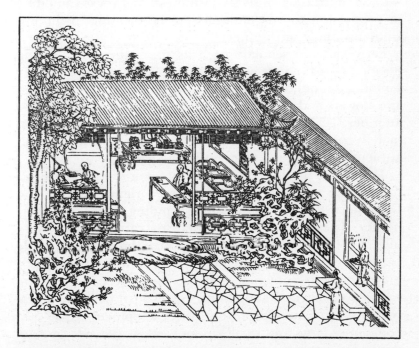

A traditional Chinese rockery using flat and curiously shaped stones in a modest Shanghai home. From a nineteenth-century print.

tains its skeleton. No surprise, then, that Feng Shui should have a special regard for all rocks. It judges their irregular shapes, formed by nature, to be good conductors of *Chi*, while in association with water they offer a way of ensuring harmony and balance in the garden.

These traditions are the *raison d'être* for rockeries, which should be designed as imitations of nature to achieve their most potent impact and, in the words of Feng Shui masters, 'by sympathetic magic confer on the garden owner a kind of immortality'.

The various old Feng Shui manuals that I have consulted suggest that there are no hard and fast rules for creating a rock garden. Evidently, centuries ago, it was realised that everything depended on a person's *innate feeling*—although it was important to strive for a natural effect and end up with an impression of stylised wildness. The rocks should be in proportion to one another and be pleasing to the eye from any angle or distance.

Early Chinese scholars such as the revered Li Li-weng decided that the best way of creating these features was by building a mound of earth on which rocks could be placed and flowers and small trees added. This not only generated an inner *Chi*, he claimed in his book *Li Yu Ch'uan-chi* (Informal Records of Random Thoughts), but also formed an attractive and unified element in the garden.

The idea of placing sculptured statues or *objects d'art* carved from stone in the garden may have originated from the Chinese custom of placing single standing stones near their homes. These rocks, either uncut or carved, which were often put beside a stately pine tree or combined with suitable beautiful flowers, were believed to bring out the very essence of nature. Equally, a small, polished rock placed in the house was said to be good Feng Shui, especially if positioned in a corner where it would prevent the development of bad *Sha*. Sometimes large and small stones were placed side by side: this was deemed to be a social symbol and would generate harmony between a master and his servants, a householder and his guests.

Feng Shui had three terms for the kind of rocks that should be used in a rockery—*t'ou, shou* and *lou*—though it must be said that, in typically enigmatic Chinese fashion, all are ambiguous:

- T'OU. This literally means 'walk through' and implies a stone with a passageway through it. A generally round stone, perhaps with a hole in it, would seem most applicable today.
- SHOU. This is a more precise word and means 'thin'. It is generally agreed to signify a delicate, feminine *Yin*-type rock.
- LOU. The most curious of all, because the word means a 'leak' or 'drip'. Today the term is said to indicate a generally rectangularly shaped rock

It must be obvious by now that in Feng Shui philosophy rocks are considered a very powerful form of energy. By incorporating them in a rockery, perhaps to build up a flat area of the garden where the *Chi* may be moving sluggishly, the whole area can be made a much more harmonious spot. The hard rocks will also contrast with the smoothness and softness of the plants and flowers growing among them to add an extra balance of *Yin* and *Yang* to the landscape.

When it comes to designing your own rockery, invention and attention to Feng Shui guidelines are all you really need. Ideally, it should be built in conjunction with a pond because the soil excavated from the ground can be used to build the mound on which the rocks are placed. If you take account of positioning and the symbolism of all the elements you use to create your own mini-mountain, then you should not go far wrong.

However, before you start, here are a few practical tips. If you have no pond, a rock garden does not have to be made in isolation: it can be part of an ordinary border and still look perfectly natural. In nature, rocks have to end somewhere and often merge into a pebbly scree which eventually becomes a loamy soil where plants and flowers grow.

A Feng Shui carved standing stone which symbolises rocks and currents of wind and water. Sketched in a Nanking garden, c.1920.

The best time to build a rockery is in the summer when the weather is fine, because it is almost impossible to do so when the soil is wet and cold. It is a good idea to draw up a rough plan of the layout before you begin and, if possible, to get hold of all the three types of stone (*t'ou, shou* and *lou*) that I have listed. There are, of course, many kinds of rock from which to choose, but Feng Shui recommends *sandstone* because there is such an attractive variety and it is easy to work with; small pieces of *granite* which have a discernible 'face'; and the harder *limestone* that weathers so beautifully. Quartz, which is often sold as a rockery stone, is actually not good because it has little shape and is generally unsympathetic to plants. Although good rocks are no cheaper to buy nowadays than they were all those centuries ago when the Chinese noblemen were squabbling over them, it is well worth purchasing fine examples, as the finished result will repay your expenditure many times over in terms of harmony and good Feng Shui.

When building your basic mound of soil, add about a fifth of fine gravel to the mixture as this will 'bulk' the mini-mountain. As you start positioning the rocks on the mound, remember that you want to create as natural an effect as possible, so never completely bury any rock and ensure that they are all in proportion with one another. The Chinese have always endeavoured to make their rock gardens look as if they had already been in existence on the land long before the house was built, and this should be your goal, too.

The stones must all be laid on the same inward-slanting plane, with about one-third of the rock buried in the mound soil. This not only makes for a pleasing natural appearance, but also enables the rain to run into the crevices where the thirsty plants are growing. Do not place rocks at different angles as this will give them an unnatural appearance and is not good Feng Shui. The distance between the rocks is obviously a matter of personal choice, but ideally they should never be more than an easy stride apart so that the plants can be tended without any being trampled.

It is important to take your time over the whole operation, to ensure that all the rocks look in harmony when the job is finished. And don't overelaborate—the Chinese kept their rock gardens simple and *never* added so many stones that they ended up with any kind of peak. A gently undulating summit is the best for the smooth passage of *Chi.* When choosing plants for a rockery, Feng Shui offers no specific recommendations, leaving the choice very much to each gardener. However, the best for this kind of feature are those which are hardy, wind-resistant, have long roots, make tight mats of foliage and produce flowers that are large in comparison to the size of the plants. My suggestion, based on good Feng Shui, would include the aquilegias, crocuses, hardy geraniums, irises, the phlox varieties, primula species, rhododendrons and all types of sedum. But at the end of the day the choice is yours.

9 *HEALTH-GIVING HERBS*

Three thousand years ago the development of Feng Shui and herbal medicine ran hand in hand in China. Magic was an important element in the Chinese attitude towards plants and trees, especially those that were found to be medically useful, so that holiness and medicinal value became linked in the people's minds. This combination of powers is probably what first stirred the aesthetic sensibilities of the herb-gatherers: a medicinal leaf, which was therefore a holy leaf, began also to be thought of as beautiful.

Exactly when the Chinese started to pursue a formal study of the nurturing qualities of their many different native herbs is impossible to guess. Certainly, it must initially have been a process of trial and error, as a result of which those herbs found most effective were cultivated for use in an ever-increasing number of medications. One of the very earliest textbooks of herbal treatments was the *Shen Nung Ben Tsao*, compiled by the legendary Emperor Shen Nung—'the divine husbandman' as he was known—who died in 2698 BC. He apparently personally sampled over one hundred herbs—and lived to a ripe old age to tell the tale—and his 'Canon of Herbs' described the properties of 252 plants, with details of how to preserve and use them. Many of Emperor Shen Nung's treatments are still in use today.

A hundred years later, herbal lore had grown to such an extent that another emperor, Huang Ti, set about formalising this knowledge in what ultimately became an 18-volume book of medicine, the *Nei Ching*. This mammoth work clearly showed that the Chinese had already realised that the distribution of nutrients was one of the functions of the blood circulating in the body. The *Nei Ching* also affirmed that it was possible for a scholar of medicine to cure all manner of illnesses by using his five senses during diagnosis, as well as by assessing a patient's breathing, pulse and skin odours. The book added, 'In treating illness, it is necessary to examine the entire context, scrutinise the symptoms, observe the emotions and attitudes. If one insists on the presence of ghosts and spirits, one cannot speak of therapeutics.'

The *Nei Ching* was updated several times in the centuries that followed, notably in the seventh century during the T'ang dynasty, when a team of twenty experts, headed by a renowned herbalist, Su Jing, surveyed all the provinces of the nation and produced a revised herbal that featured over eight hundred herbs. This book was thereafter printed and distributed throughout China—600 years before the first Western printing press was even invented.

In 1578, during the Ming dynasty, a Chinese doctor named Li Shizhen (1518–93), having spent 27 years travelling about the nation, collecting and testing remedies, published his *Ben Ts'ao Kang Mu* (the 'Compendium of Materia Medica') in which he listed a total of 1,173 healing plants and 11,000 recipes and compounds. Again, many of the herbs Li Shizhen noted down are still in use today, while the search for still more goes on. In the last quarter of a century, for example, the Chinese have collected and identified a further 2,000 medicinal herbs, with no sign of the end in sight.

Right from those far-off days when the principles of Feng Shui were being developed, the early *xiansheng*, too, appreciated the value of herbs in generating good health and promoting a sense of well-being. Consequently, they were soon advocating the cultivation of selected herbs which they believed were good for attaining harmony as well as encouraging the circulation of *Chi* within a house and garden. This concept mirrored the Chinese vision of the after-life as a garden full of beautiful, useful plants influential to all aspects of life.

Although there is clearly no difficulty in seeing the physical differences between herbs and flowers and trees, Feng Shui from the very start did not set out to divide them into separate groups; it believed there was a place for all three in the harmonious garden. Indeed, historical documents show that the earliest gardens in places such as the Summer Palaces in Peking and Kunming, the 'city of eternal spring' (both of which were constructed according to Feng Shui principles), contained a mixture of herbs growing among various kinds of flora. In both palaces, willow, maple and apricot trees kept company with peonies, roses and lotus flowers, and interspersed between them grew such herbs as chives, saffron, ginseng and tea chrysanthemums.

Interestingly, the leaves and young stems of one species of chrysanthemum, known as *Hao zi gan*, are still in everyday use in China. They are used raw in salads, as a flavouring in soup and as a vegetable—albeit one with a humble status as its European name 'chop suey' greens implies ('chop suey', the anglicised form of the Chinese *za cui*, refers to the boiled leftovers from a restaurant which are usually given to the poor). Notwithstanding this reputation, the greens have a distinct, tangy flavour, are succulent and nutritious, and are said to be rich in vitamins and minerals. The chrysanthemum petals can also be used fresh or dried, as a garnish or sprinkled over soups or salads, although the centre is best avoided as it can leave a bitter aftertaste.

When contemplating making a herb garden, the advice of Feng Shui is to be informal and devise an area in which circular shapes predominate in order that the *Chi* will flow smoothly. You should also concentrate on growing those herbs whose 'magic powers' create harmony and beauty as well as being useful to the household. There is no need to separate the culinary and medicinal herbs, for the ancient art

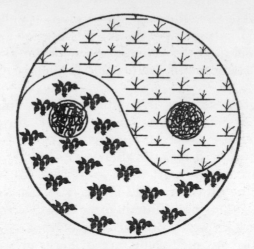

A *Yin* and *Yang* herb bed.

regards them as ideal partners like *Yin* and *Yang*, providing a variety of shapes and colours. Because the Chinese never set out to create domestic herb gardens such as those which later evolved in the West, there are no specific models to follow and invention is yet again the keyword in your Feng Shui gardening. Where the Chinese *have* excelled is in creating areas where peace, privacy and harmony combine through the use of different textures of light and shade and the comforting aroma of herbs.

I have already emphasised how opposed Feng Shui is to sharp corners and walled-off areas. It also disapproves of the kind of regimented herb beds found in the monastery gardens of the Middle Ages or the orderly kitchen gardens of the Victorians. Instead, choose a circular or curved shape for your herb bed, such as the four typical examples I have illustrated here.

1　The *Yin* and *Yang* herbal bed. This is the most basic Feng Shui herb 'garden' and also the easiest to maintain. Based on the age-old symbol, each half should be given over to a favourite low-lying herb, with the 'eyes' represented by a small circle of a slightly taller plant such as chives or

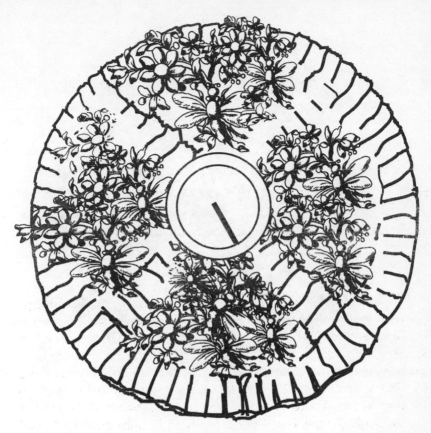

The herb clock.

coriander. But do remember it is bad Feng Shui to use more than two different herbs *per half*.

2 The *herb clock* has become quite a favourite with expatriate Chinese families living in the Far East and America. The outline can be made with bricks or stone slabs (or turf) and each segment of soil should contain a single different type of herb. Some followers of Feng Shui believe that a central feature like a rounded plinth or small pagoda—certainly nothing angular—will help the flow of the *Chi*.

3 The *cartwheel* herb 'garden' has been successfully developed in Hong Kong, Singapore and even in several Australian cities where there are numbers of Chinese resi-

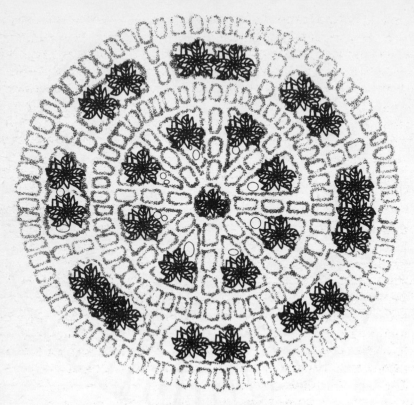

The cartwheel.

dents. Each segment should contain a different herb, and Feng Shui says it is advisable to start by planting the inner wheel before adding the outer circles. The nice thing about this type is that you can go on adding new rings of herbs so long as you have the space.

4 The *Chi* 'garden' is the most complex of all and requires a fairly sizeable piece of land. The design of the sweeping path is symbolic of the flow of the *Chi* and by its very nature will allow the earth energies to pass smoothly through the area, carrying with them the aromas of the herbs right to the centre point of the little pond. The number of herbs is entirely at your discretion, but those around the path should be low-growing types, with taller varieties behind

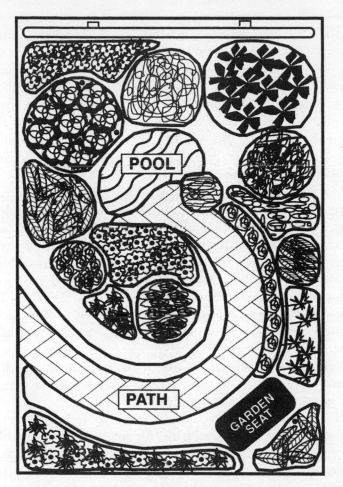

Plan of a herb garden.

the pool. This layout can be finished off by placing a small seat or bench on the centre of the curve facing towards the water feature, and here you will be able to pass many happy hours while the *Chi* is wafting the fragrance of the herbs all around you. (It has been suggested to me that the really adventurous gardener might like to use the Feng Shui *bagua* (see p. 48) as a model for a herb garden, with the plants arranged in the shapes of the eight trigrams: but I was warned that it would be no easy undertaking.)

The ideal location for a Feng Shui herb garden is the tiger (right-hand side) of the garden where the low-lying, intense energy of the plants is most appropriate for the whole area. Do not be over-ambitious in choosing your design (you can always be bolder once you have succeeded with the basics) and look for a position that is well drained and enjoys full sun for at least two-thirds of the day. Decide whether you want the bed near the kitchen for ease of access (and the opportunity for the *Chi* and the aromas to drift indoors) or farther away as a kind of retreat.

Many herbs need protection from the winds, which is why Feng Shui has always advocated growing them in the lee of larger plants or trees. If this is impossible, erect some bamboo fencing or trelliswork that will concentrate the fragrance of the herbs as well as providing a feeling of seclusion. Remember that, like everything else in the garden, this spot must be in harmony and balance with the rest of the landscape. The sizes and shapes of the herbs should also be complementary, and it is a good idea to site annuals so that you will not risk disturbing perennials when planting or removing them. In short, go for an effect that intermingles flowers, plants and herbs in a natural manner that will generate good Feng Shui for you all year round.

If you live in a flat or small apartment without a garden, but do have a small patio or balcony, it is still possible to benefit from the harmonious properties of herbs by planting a group of them in containers. They will not only bring beauty and aromatic smells into your world, but by carefully positioning the pots you can use them to soften the harsh angles of a walled yard or balcony to facilitate the smooth flow of the *Chi* in and out of the home.

Herbs are very well suited to being grown in containers because most of them will flourish in well-drained soil. They are also a boon to the town-dweller because they scent the air, generate produce for the kitchen and can be decorative into the bargain. Furthermore, by choosing a selection of containers—terracotta pots, old chimney pots, glazed sinks and traditional garden and kitchen containers, all of which make excellent growers—and by planting a variety of bushy or trailing herbs in them, a picturesque garden can be created in even the smallest corner.

Space can also be maximised if the containers are of varying sizes and not all stood on the floor—for example, put some of them on a window-sill or shelf, and hang others from a wall. And of course they can all be moved about at a moment's notice to create a completely fresh arrangement without all the bother of transplanting. Make sure, however, that the pots are always somewhere sunny and bright and do not form a barrier against the *Chi*. They should also be sheltered from draughts and extremes of temperature in order to encourage growth and, in specific cases, the production of aromatic oils which can bring another element of delight into your life.

A Feng Shui herb garden should be a picture of beauty and informality, featuring plants of all shapes and sizes—though never too many as profusion leads to confusion and will hamper the flow of the *Chi*.

To help you in your selection, here is a list of the herbs recommended by Feng Shui for their special contributions to the balance and harmony of a garden.

FENG SHUI HERBS

Chinese chives (Dahsuahn) *Allium tuberosum*
Element: *Yin*
Symbolism: *Appetite*
For centuries the Chinese have referred to the onion family as the 'jewels among vegetables' and regard them as having exceptional health-giving properties—the stronger the smell, they say, the more effective the healing powers. Chinese chives comes at the top of this list and has been favourably mentioned in the country's records for the last 3,000 years. It was Marco Polo who first brought news of Chinese chives to the West, and it is probably true to say that its light, garlic-type flavour is now an essential ingredient in many soups and salads where its iron and vitamin content

stimulates the appetite and aids digestion. Feng Shui believes that the plant is not only good at combating the build-up of *Sha* in a garden, but also makes an ideal partner when planted near new roses (it will enhance their scent) and under a peach tree (where it will control leaf curl.) *A. tuberosum* grows in clumps up to 50cm (20ins) tall in sunny, well-drained positions. It has flat green leaves and attractive terminal clusters of white, starry, sweet-scented flowers that bloom in the late spring. After blooming, the flowers should be removed and the leaves cut to within 5cm (2ins) of the ground to allow for regrowth. Chinese chives can be propagated by seed sown between October and April or by root division in the autumn or spring. The herb can also be potted up and grown indoors for a winter supply of chives. Feng Shui says that apart from its place in the herb garden, *A. tuberosum* can also be used as attractive ground cover, and is a good component of an all-white flowerbed, as well as being a highlight in a mixed perennial border.

Cinnamon (Dan) *Cinnamomum zeylanicum*
Element: *Yin*
Symbolism: *Rejuvenation*
Sometimes referred to as Chinese cinnamon or, occasionally, 'Canton Cassia' (after *Cinnamomum cassia*, a species that is less delicate and with not such a good smell), this herb has been used in China primarily as a tonic and as a flavour for other medicine, rather than—as in the West—to scent pot-pourri and to flavour drinks and foods. Cinnamon is an evergreen tree which grows to about 6m (20ft), with a thick, leathery bark and small white flowers which produce oval, bluish-coloured fruits. All three are fragrant, but it is the dried inner bark of the branches which is used as a spice in wines, teas, honey and cooked fruit. The ground seeds provide the raw materials for pot-pourri and perfume oil. To grow cinnamon in the West, it is best put in pure sand in a warm, sheltered spot and constantly watered. This makes it a good choice for the corner of a covered patio, and there it will also serve effectively as a conductor of *Chi* in and out of the house.

Coriander (Hursuei) *Coriandrum sativum*
Element: *Yin*
Symbolism: *Longevity*
The Chinese were probably among the first of the ancient civilisations to discover that the coriander, which grew wild in their country, could be used in cooking and medicine. Indeed, such was the power accorded to the herb that for many years the people even believed that it conferred immortality on those who drank it mixed in pure, fresh water. Feng Shui lore particularly admires the curved and tangled branches of the plant which mean that it is a good conductor of *Chi* wherever it is positioned. *C. sativum* likes to be in full sun in a rich, well-drained soil and can be sown from seed in early spring. The thin, bright green upper leaves of the herb have a pungent smell, while the lower ones are broader and have a taste like aromatic parsley, which is why the plant is sometimes referred to as 'Chinese parsley'. The flowers are white or pale purple and blossom from early to midsummer. The lower leaves can be picked at any time and used fresh in stews, salads, sauces and as a garnish; but the seeds, which have many uses in vegetable dishes, curries, fruit pies and cakes, should be collected when they have turned brown and must be dried before use. The roots, which should be dug up in the autumn, can be cooked as a vegetable and also used in curries.

Ginseng (Jen shen) *Panax quinquefolius*
Element: *Yang*
Symbolism: *Health*
The root of this species of ginseng, which is not unlike that of the mandrake, is often referred to in its native China as 'man's health' and has been highly valued for centuries. When first discovered in Manchuria, such were the health-giving properties ascribed to it that for generations the Emperor and members of his court took first claim on all the ginseng that was grown, and the rest of the population were forced to go in search of supplies wherever they could. Feng Shui believes ginseng is important to a garden not just

because of its health-giving roots, but because of the stems which it grows above ground. Initially, the plant puts out one stem bearing five leaves; subsequently a second stem with the same number of leaves, then a third, and later a fourth when it begins to grow a stalk from the middle which is referred to in Chinese as 'the hundred feet'. These willowy stems are excellent conductors of *Chi* and are made all the more so by the pale lilac flowers with their filaments that resemble untwisted silk. The ginseng grows to 30–45cm (12–18ins) and likes a humus-rich soil in shade. The herb is best started in a greenhouse before being transplanted outside and will be ready for harvesting after about three years. The many uses of the ginseng root in generating good health, fighting depression, giving relief from nausea and easing coughs and chest disorders, have been too well documented to need repeating in these pages.

Marsh mallow (Jiinkveir) *Althaea chinensis*
Element: *Yin*
Symbolism: *Sweetness*
This mallow, which is one of hundreds of species of the Malvaceae family, is also known as the 'Chinese mallow' and is the original source of inspiration for the delicious sweet-meat of the same name. It comes from the root of the plant which was found, when powdered, to contain a mucilage that thickened with water and sugar to create a sweet mixture which rapidly acquired popularity. Do not imagine, though, that a garden full of marsh mallow plants will enable you to make plates of marshmallow sweets like those sold at the confectioner's: the only thing they have in common with the original recipe is the sugar! However, the herb, with its large, velvety leaves and pink or white flowers with their attractive purple stamens, which appear from late summer to early autumn, are good circulators of *Chi* in the garden. The plant, which grows to a height of 2m (6ft), should be sown in spring in a sunny position with good soil. The young leaves may be used fresh in salads, as can the ripened light brown seeds. After digging up and drying, the roots should be

steeped in water for eight hours or else boiled to release the mucilage, at this is said to be good for dry skin and hair. Feng Shui considers this hardy mallow good for border planting; it has a subtle and comforting fragrance which is released into the air in warm weather.

Pennyroyal (Lintsas) *Mentha pulegium*
Element: *Yang*
Symbolism: *Warm feelings*
Pennyroyal has had a double role in Chinese society for centuries: as a medicine and as a token of hospitality to relatives and friends visiting a home. Of the many species of mint now grown in the West, *M. pulegium* is known to have originated from a species that first grew in northern China. Feng Shui favours this species because it weaves its way close to the ground and is very beneficial to the smooth flow of *Chi.* The bright-green leaves with their unmistakable peppermint scent grow on creeping stems which root quickly wherever they make contact with the soil. The pennyroyal is happy in sun or partial shade and likes rich, well-drained soil. It can be grown from root or stem cuttings in spring, and its leaves should be picked just before flowering. An aromatic and convivial herb in the garden, its uses in the house are many–a refreshing tea, a deterrent to ants and fleas in cupboards, and an oil (which the Chinese call *Po Ho*) to massage rheumatic and muscular aches. To many Feng Shui gardeners, no herb bed would be complete without the pennyroyal.

Sage (Jer) *Salvia officinalis*
Element: *Yang*
Symbolism: *Esteem/longevity*
The sage is another essential herb in China, and the people have an ancient proverb, much quoted, which says, 'How can a man grow old who has sage in his garden?' The plant is said to contain the power of longevity, is a wonderful healer and has many culinary uses. Feng Shui goes farther and says that its shape is conducive to the *Chi*, its aroma is

good for harmony, and as a flowering garden plant it is a match for many other blooms. Sometimes referred to in China as *Tan-shan*, the sage has been a favoured plant in rock gardens for centuries because of its ability to thrive in heat and drought. It flourishes in light, dry soil and full sun. *S. officinalis* can be grown from cuttings and will root within a month in the summer. However, it can become large and woody and requires pruning to keep its shape and balance within the garden. The grey-green, downy leaves should be picked before the mauve-blue, deep-throated flowers appear, and these should be thoroughly dried in order to make them especially aromatic and pungent. Sage can, of course, be used in many ways: as a mix for stuffing, as a deodorant for cooking and animal smells; as a cleaning agent for face and teeth; and as an antiseptic and aid to digestion. Feng Shui says the best position for sage is at the front of a herb bed or garden border.

Vervain (Lurngyar) *Verbena officinalis*
Element: *Yang*
Symbolism: *Enchantment*
Vervain has a special place in Feng Shui because of its association with the dragon, and it is known to many Chinese as 'dragon-teeth grass'—which hints that the plant has hidden powers when properly used. Indeed it does, for its ridged, dark green stem, pale lilac flowers and distinctive leaves (they are rather like elongated versions of our oak leaf) are all excellent conductors of *Chi*. Feng Shui manuals sometimes refer to this herb as 'iron vervain' in tribute to its medicinal powers and qualities as a massage infusion. The plant has also earned a reputation as an aphrodisiac (an old English name for vervain, 'enchanter's plant', seems to lend credence to this claim), and there is no doubt that for many years it has been mixed in Chinese love potions and added to exotic dishes and alcoholic drinks. Vervain is a hardy herbaceous perennial that grows to up to 1m (3ft) tall and should be sown in spring in a fertile, well-drained, sunny part of the garden. The leaves may be picked as required,

and the whole plant can be preserved for making into a liquid for treating bruises or a sedative nightcap. Vervain can also be grown indoors, and whether there, or in a bed near the house, it will add an extra element of enchantment to the *Chi* as it wafts into the home.

10 *THE GROWTH OF 'HARMONY GARDENING'*

The Emperor Huang Ti is said to have been one of the founders of the nation's husbandry and medicinal botany. He is reputed to have invented the plough, tested different kinds of soils to discover which crops would grow best in them, and instituted the ceremonies for sowing various seeds, plants and flowers at the most propitious times of the year. As described in chapter 9, he is also believed to have written a pharmacopoeia which later formed the basis of the great book of herbal medicine, the *Ben-T'sao*, which was assembled by Li Shizhen between 1560 and 1590.

Although it seems likely that Huang Ti utilised a number of the existing principles of Feng Shui in his horticulture, it was not until the reign of the Han Emperor Wu-ti (140–86 BC) that we find documentary evidence of the ancient art being employed on his land to facilitate growth. It seems that Wu-ti was so keen on gardening that he dispatched a small army of servants all over China to collect herbaceous plants, tees and flowers for his collection. One of his gardens, with its own summer palace, several pavilions, and any number of floral areas, lakes and rockeries, is said to have covered an area of over 50 square miles. Today the memory of the emperor is held in high esteem because of his horticultural achievements: he began the system for defining the different varieties of flowers and introduced into common cultivation such plants as beans, coriander and even the grape-vine. His example was followed by a number of rich men who began landscaping their estates, and later poets, painters and scholars all added their own contributions to the theory and practice of garden design.

However, the use of Feng Shui in gardening really began to flourish in China during the T'ang dynasty. It was then that the nobility started to expand their gardens by commandeering the land of the farming people, to such an extent that only a peasant uprising put a halt to the worst excesses. But nothing could halt the inexorable rise of Chinese garden art, and during the T'ang dynasty (AD 618–906) and those that followed—the Sung, Yuan and Ming dynasties—it developed to its highest point as the Chinese people grew ever more certain that their fortunes were intimately affected by the landscape in which they lived.

A famous story is told of the T'ang Emperor Hui-tsung who, although he was then only 26, was disturbed by the fact that he had no sons. He instructed a group of Feng Shui *xiansheng* to examine the imperial city, and after deliberating, their advice was that the land round about was too flat: the emperor could not have male heirs while the land to the north-east of the capital especially was so low-lying. The emperor at once ordered a mountain to be built, which he was informed would block out the evil forces, concentrate the good *Chi*, and enable him to have male children. Although Hui-tsung did, indeed, father the heir he desired, the enormous cost of building the mountain, which was named *Ken-yu*, brought down the dynasty in financial ruin.

Tales of these traditions filtered back to the West by means of visiting missionaries and intrepid travellers, to influence not only English landscaping and the *jardins chinois-anglais*, but ultimately the modern gardens of northern Europe and America. Along with other elements of Chinese culture, the garden had also been imported into Japan in the eighth century, where its veneration of nature-mysticism was reinforced by Zen-Buddhism with its own cult of the mini-mountain and lotus pool.

The thinking behind all this nature-mysticism had been defined long before by a Chinese writer, Lien-Tschen, who wrote:

> The art of laying gardens consists in an endeavour to combine cheerfulness of aspect, luxuriance of growth, shade, solitude and repose in such a manner that the senses may be deluded by an imitation of rural nature. Diversity, which is the main advantage of natural landscape, must therefore be sought by a judicious choice of soil, an alternation of chains of hills and valleys, and brooks and lakes covered with water plants. Symmetry is wearisome, and ennui and disgust will soon be excited in a garden where every part betrays constraint and artificiality.

The Chinese believed that gardens were essentially places in which to think, to withdraw from the stresses and strains of the world. Nothing in them must be allowed to encourage haste or promote anything that was blatant. Paths were not intended to provide access from one point to another, but the opportunity to enjoy at leisure every view and mood of the landscape, so they were all made deliberately winding. The natural landscapes that the Chinese most admired were, as we know, mountains and hills, running streams and water pools. And because they saw their gardens as creations of the mind, they imitated nature on whatever scale best suited their requirements, through the use of a few well-positioned rocks, a pool of water, and the careful cultivation of all sorts of plants.

One result of this 'miniaturising' of a landscape—often based on an area beloved by the owner—was that every element was believed to have a meaning and its own symbolism. 'Herbs and trees, stones and rocks shall all enter into heaven', runs an old Chinese proverb, which helps to explain

just *why* every element in a Feng Shui garden was thought to
have its own vivid personality. The sum total of this dedicated
husbandry was to bring man into harmony with nature,
a state that would render him immune from evil and bad
luck.

For many centuries the gardens of China were secret
places from which the 'barbarians and foreign devils were
excluded', so any reports of them prior to the last two hundred years are few and far between. We do know, however,
that many historic gardens existed in the country: one
famous example which dates back to a time shortly before
the Christian era was that of the Emperor Wu-ti of Han who
had a vast pleasure garden called the *Shang Lin*, or Royal
Park. Several cities in the heartlands of China were also
famous for their gardens, including Nanking, Soochow and
Hangchow. Shanghai boasted the *Yu Yuan*, or Garden of
Ease, of which a contemporary record states, 'Within are
terraces, pools, rocks, flowers and bamboos; it is very beautiful and no other garden within the district can compare with
it.' This same account adds that the five features mentioned
are considered the 'pillars of a garden' upon which every
other element relies, the last being especially important. 'If
there arc no bamboos then the people are uncultivated,
untutored,' it declares unequivocally.

Later, the Emperor Ch'ien-lung would declare that all
trees and flowers were not just illustrative of a person's feelings, but in some sense the source of them. He wrote, 'When
I find pleasure in orchids, I love uprightness; when I see
pines and bamboos I think of virtue; when I stand beside a
stream I value honesty; when I see weeds I despise dishonesty.
That is what is meant by the proverb, "The Ancients get
their ideas from objects".'

The first complete description of a Chinese garden to
reach the West was that of a French Jesuit, Père Attivet, who
was allowed entry to the gardens of the Emperor Chi'ien-
lung in Peking in 1749. Known as the *Yuan Ming Yuan* or
'Garden of Perfect Brightness', it seemed to its visitor one
of the most fantastic gardens that had ever been built. The

priest's letter, sent back to Paris and published there, described it as a place in which the emperor and his courtiers could relax, which was apparently haphazardly filled with flowers in curved beds, weirdly shaped trees and curiously shaped rocks. The whole garden was surrounded by a high wall decorated with little pictures which Père Attivet was not to learn until later were Feng Shui symbols.

In the fullness of time the Jesuit's letter, and others that followed, launched a revolution in garden taste in the West, away from the traditional straight lines and right-angled corners. A number of wealthy European landowners attempted to model their gardens on what they had read about those in China, and although they knew little or nothing about the philosophy of Feng Shui, a few of them seem to have unconsciously embraced its philosophy, as shown in the sketch opposite of an elaborately laid-out garden in Alsatia dating from the late nineteenth century. The house, which belonged to the postmaster of Allkirch, faced over a pool of water towards a rockery of plants and shrubs interspersed with shady walks. Beyond these lay 'some of the grandest prospects of the Rhine and Alps', according to a contemporary account. Perfect Feng Shui!

When visitors from the West began to gain access to China in ever-increasing numbers—especially during the Victorian era—many were deeply impressed by the gardens they saw, though they were quite evidently unaware of the principles that had governed their design. Sir William Chambers, a surveyor who spent several years in China, wrote in his *Dissertation on Oriental Gardening* (1850):

Nature is the model of the Chinese, but their aim appears to be to imitate her only in her irregularities. As the Chinese are not fond of walking, we rarely find avenues or broad gravel walks in their gardens. And their grounds, however extensive they may be, are broken up into a variety of small scenes, each perfect in itself, but so totally unconnected with every thing around it. When they find this irregular beauty in per-

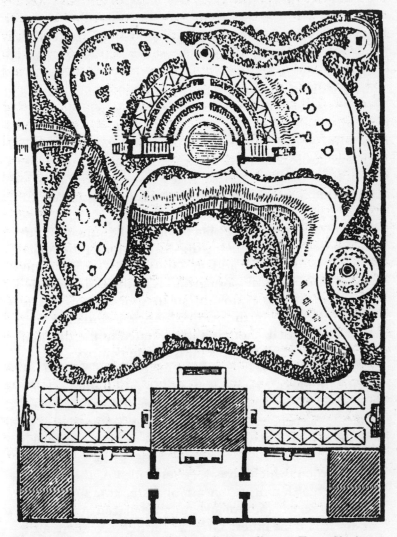

Plan of a German garden designed according to Feng Shui principles, with curved pathways, semi-circular lines of shrubs and circular flowerbeds. Late nineteenth century.

fection, so as to hit the eye, they say it is *shanawadgi*—
an expression signifying fine or admirable.

Although he did not realise it, Sir William had actually mis-
heard the expression: what he imagined was *shanawadgi* was
actually 'Feng Shui'.

Another English writer of the time, J. C. Loudon, compiled
The Encyclopaedia of Gardening (1860), a massively detailed
study of horticulture and landscape gardening around the
world, 'With Suggestions for its Future Progress in the British
Isles' (to quote the sub-heading). In it he illustrated a suburban villa 'in the Chinese style' (see engraving), which
belonged to a wealthy merchant in Canton, and wrote of it:

> We do not present the villa as one to be imitated; but
> the gardener, by observing the distribution of the rocks,
> the vases of plants, and the trees, may derive many
> useful hints for laying out grounds in the Chinese style,
> or for making the most of small spots in town. The
> vases of flowers in the garden were continually being
> changed; so that, though it was situated in the midst of
> a town, it had all the freshness of the country.

Probably the first Western writer to describe the practice of
Feng Shui gardening in any detail was a Frenchman named
Olivier de Serres, writing in the *Gardener's Magazine* of June
1890 about a garden which he had recently visited in Peking:

> This garden, which gives a general idea of the style of
> Chinese gardening as an art of taste, contained only
> twenty acres of land. An apartment is placed at the head
> of its useful beauties. On the south were seen little
> cascades and hedges of roses and pomegranate trees;
> on the west, a solitary portico, evergreen trees, a
> meadow, sheets of water surrounded with turf and a
> labyrinth of rocks; on the north, some edifices placed
> as if by chance on little hills and groves of bamboos
> with gravel walks; on the east, a small plain of odorifer-

The garden of a wealthy Feng Shui devotee in Canton, from a Chinese engraving made in 1860. Notice the use of trelliswork on the house and garden walls, and the container plants placed among the trees.

ous plants, medicinal plants, shrubs, citron and orange trees, a walk of willows, bridges of wood and stone, a pond, some old firs and an extensive view across the surrounding countryside. The laying out of these gardens, I was told, was crystallised under the laws of Feng Shui which the Chinese have observed since ancient times and in which they place great faith.

The twentieth century has seen a growing interest in Chinese gardens in the West, typified by such groundbreaking articles as Florence Ayscough's 'The Chinese Idea of a Garden', published in *The China Journal of Sciences* in June 1923, and Grace M. Boynton's 'Notes on the Origins of Chinese Gardens' in *The China Journal* (July 1935). These were followed by a number of books, including Dorothy Graham's *Chinese Gardens* (1938), *Chinese Houses and Gardens* by Henry Inn and S. C. Lu (1940), *Gardens of China* by Osvald Siren (1949), Ernest H. Wilson's *China: Mother of Gardens* (1971) and *The Gardens of China: Art, Architecture and Meanings* by Edwin T. Morris (1984). All of these have been useful in my research and each mentions the influence of Feng Shui in Chinese gardening without going into the detail I have attempted in these pages. But together with the help of personal contacts, these books and articles have helped to show me that Feng Shui gardens are, in effect, cosmic diagrams which reveal an ancient and very profound view of the world and our place in it. All their elements are designed to flow with the soft curves of nature and provide havens of inner strength for men and women so that they might harmonise with the passing seasons. Yet for all the guidance that is available, it is clear that there are really no hard and fast rules in planning such a garden—it is more important to rely on your surroundings, your emotions, and the *suggestions* the ancient art has to make.

It is undoubtedly an ongoing tradition, too. Feng Shui gardening has much to offer people in this modern technological and increasingly frenetic world. The garden has always been a source of comfort to mankind, and with the help of this time-honoured philosophy it can become a place that offers still more in the way of harmony and well-being. Nor should I underestimate the sights, sounds and fragrances that will bring a little of the mysterious and magical East into any country home, suburban house or even tiny city flat. Armed with what has been explained in these pages, I hope that readers will be prepared to try. Good luck, good gardening—and especially, good Feng Shui!

BIBLIOGRAPHY AND USEFUL ADDRESSES

Beales, Peter. *Classic Roses*, 2nd ed. (London, 1997).

Beckett, Kenneth A., Carr, David and Stevens, David. *The Contained Garden* (London, 1982).

Brickell, Christopher (ed.). *The RHS A-Z Encyclopedia of Garden Plants* (London, 1996).

Chi Ch'eng. *Yuan Yeh* (reissue, Peking, 1933).

Cox, E.H.M. *Plant Hunting in China* (London, 1945).

Danby, Hope. *The Garden of Perfect Brightness* (London, 1950).

Dyer, T.F. Thiselton. *The Folklore of Plants* (New York, 1889).

Fisher, Sue. *The Complete Book of Water Gardens* (London, 1994).

Fisk, Jim. *Clematis: The Queen of Climbers* (London, 1989).

Fu Weikang. *Traditional Chinese Medicine* (Beijing, 1985).

Garland, Sarah. *The Herb Garden* (London, 1984).

Goldsmith, H.T.J. and Backhurst, A.E. *Market Gardening in China* (London, 1986).

Howard, Edwin. *Chinese Garden Architecture* (New York, 1931).

Kelly, John. *Planning and Planting Rock Gardens* (Newton Abbott, 1994).

Kerby, Kate. *An Old Chinese Garden* (Shanghai, 1922).

Keys, John D. *Chinese Herbs* (Los Angeles, 1976).

King, F.H. *Farmers of Forty Centuries* (New York, 1911).

Larkcom, Joy. *Planning the Organic Herb Garden* (London, 1986)..

Li, H.I. *The Garden Flowers of China* (New York, 1959).

McHoy, Peter. *Containers and Baskets for All Year Round* (London, 1993).

Murck, Alfreda and Wen Feng. *A Chinese Garden Court* (New York, 1970).

Page, Martin. *The Gardener's Guide to Growing Peonies* (Newton Abbott, 1997).

Quin Yun. *Classical Chinese Gardens* (Hong Kong, 1977).

Swindells, Philip. *Garden Pools, Waterfalls and Fountains*, 2nd ed. (London, 1995).

Thomas, Graham Stuart. *Climbing Roses Old and New*, rev. ed. (London, 1983).

——. *The Old Shrub Roses*, rev. ed. (London, 1979).

Toogood, Alan, *Garden Trees Handbook* (London, 1990).

Trehane, David. *A Plantsman's Guide to Camellias* (London, 1989).

T'ung Chu-in. *Chinese Gardens* (Hong Kong, 1936).

Verey, Rosemary. *The Scented Garden* (reissue, London, 1995).

Weng Wan-go. *Gardens in Chinese Art* (New York, 1968).

Wilson, Andrew. *The Creative Water Garden* (London, 1995).

SUPPLIERS

Plants, Tree and Shrubs

Jacques Amand, The Nurseries, Clamp Hill, Stanmore, Middlesex HA7 3JS. Tel: 0181 427 3968. (*lilies*)

David Austin Roses, Bowling Green Lane, Albrighton, Wolverhampton WV7 3HB. Tel: 01902 375028. (*old roses*)

Peter Beales Roses, London Road, Attleborough, Norfolk NR17 1AY. Tel: 01953 454707. (*old roses*)

Chris Bowers & Sons, Whispering Trees Nurseries, Wimbotsham, Norfolk PE34 8QB. (*trees*)

Beth Chatto, White Barn House, Elmstead Market, Colchester, Essex CO7 7DB. (*border plants*)

Hillier Nurseries (Winchester) Ltd., Romsey Road, Winchester, Hampshire SO22 5DN. (*trees and shrubs*)

Iden Croft Herbs, Frittenden Road, Staplehurst, Kent TN12 0DH. Tel: 01580 891432. (*herbs*)

Jungle Giants, Wigmore, Herefordshire HR6 9QW. Tel: 01568 770 708. (*bamboos*)

Scotts Nurseries (Merriott) Ltd., Crewkerne, Somerset TA16 5PL. (*trees, shrubs and plants*)

Seeds

Great Britain

Boyce Seeds, Bush Pasture, Lower Carter Street, Fordham, Cambridge CB7 5JU.

D.T. Brown & Co. Ltd., Station Road, Poulton-le-Fylde, Lancashire FY6 7HX. Tel: 01253 882371

Chiltern Seeds, Bortree Stile, Ulverston, Cumbria CB7 5JU. Tel: 01229 581137

Dobies Seeds, Broomhill Way, Torquay, Devon TQ2 7QW. Tel: 01803 616888

Johnsons Seeds, Boston, Lincolnshire PE21 8AD.

Mr Fothergill's Seeds, Kentford, Newmarket, Suffolk CB8 7QB. Tel: 01638 552512

Suttons Seeds, Hele Road, Torquay, Devon TQ2 7QJ.

Thompson & Morgan, Poplar Lane, Ipswich, Suffolk IP8 3BU. Tel: 01473 688588

Unwins Seeds, Impington Lane, Histon, Cambridge CB4 4LE.

United States

Bountiful Gardens, 5798 Ridgewood Road, Willits, California 95490.

Johnny's Selected Seeds, Foss Hill Road, Albion, Maine 04910.

Nichols Rare Seeds, 1190 North Pacific Highway, Albany, Oregon 97321.

Seeds Blum, Idaho City Stage, Boise, Idaho 83706.

Shepherd's Garden Seeds, 6116 Highway 9, Felton, California 95018.

Vermont Seed Co., Garden Lane, Fair Haven, Vermont 07543.

Australia and New Zealand

Kings Herb Seeds, PO Box 14, Glenbrook, NSW 2773, Australia.

Somerset Cottage, 745 Old Northern Road, Dural, NSW 2158, Australia.

Herb Trust, 120 McCormacks Bay Road, Christchurch 8, New Zealand.

Pond Liners

Wight Butyl Liners Ltd., Market Square, St Neots, Cambridge PE19 2BG.

CPS Aquatic, Freepost, Langford, Biggleswade, Bedfordshire SG18 9GP.

Water Garden Products

Bradshaws Pumps and Filters, Freepost 56 Nicolson Link, Clifton Moor, York YO1 1SS.

Stapeley Water Gardens Ltd., London Road, Stapeley, Nantwich, Cheshire CW5 7LH.

Wychwood Aquatic Plants, Farnham Road, Odiham, nr. Basingstoke, Hampshire RG25 1HS.

INDEX